History & Historiography:
From Ancient to Modern World

History & Historiography: From Ancient to Modern World

Editors

Ashu J

&

Srotoswini Borah

Vij Books India Pvt Ltd
New Delhi (India)

Published by

Vij Books India Pvt Ltd
(Publishers, Distributors & Importers)
2/19, Ansari Road
Delhi – 110 002
Phones: 91-11-43596460, 91-11-47340674
e-mail: vijbooks@rediffmail.com
web : www.vijbooks.com

First Published in India in 2018

Copyright © 2018, Editors

ISBN: 978-93-88161-02--2 (Paperback)
ISBN: 978-93-88161-03-9 (ebook)

All rights reserved.

No part of this book may be reproduced, stored in a retrieval system, transmitted or utilized in any form or by any means, electronic, mechanical, photocopying, recording or otherwise, without the prior permission of the copyright owner. Application for such permission should be addressed to the publisher.

The views expressed in this book are of the authors/contributors in their personal capacity and do not represent the views of the institution they belong to.

Dedicated to
Our Parents, Beloved Ones, Friends
and Our Well-wishers

Contents

Foreword — xi

Preface — xiii

Acknowledgement — xv

Introduction — 1

Section — I : Ancient History

CHAPTER – ONE — 9

Climatic Changes in the Pre and Proto Historical Periods: An Emphasis on the Natural Factors

Ashu J

CHAPTER – TWO — 14

Beginning of Iron Age in India and its Extension

Srotoswini Borah

CHAPTER – THREE — 19

Buddhism: It's Emergence & Popularity in Early India

Bitumani Tahbildar & Srotoswini Borah

CHAPTER – FOUR — 29

Buddhist Theory of Kingship in Aggañña Sutta of Dīgha Nikāya

Prabira Sethy

CHAPTER – FIVE 66

The Problem of Dīdārgañj Caurī Bearer's Identification – A Response

Kanika Gupta

CHAPTER – SIX 77

Gender Depiction in Visual Art

Apeksha Gandotra

Section — II : Medieval History

CHAPTER – SEVEN 83

The Interconnection between History and Literature

Vandana Rana

CHAPTER – EIGHT 92

Understanding the Rise of Mongol Military Power and its Implications on Research

TCA Achintya

CHAPTER – NINE 105

Historical Consciousness in Pre Modern India

Vandana Rana

Section —III : Modern History

CHAPTER – TEN 113

The Influence of Ancient Rome on the French Revolution and its Potential for Class Analysis

TCA Achintya

CHAPTER – ELEVEN 125

Development of Indian Archaeology till the Close of the 19th Century

    Srotoswini Borah

CHAPTER – TWELVE 133

Archaeology and Museums: Rethinking Sense of Identity in India

    Rajeev Kumar

CHAPTER – THIRTEEN 146

Journey towards Modern India: Indira Priyadarshini Gandhi the Creator of Modern India

    Ashu J

Contributors 153

Index 157

Foreword

History had remained an integral part for several studies, however our knowledge towards history is very limited and we are still in the process of learning new aspects from our past. The idea of publishing this book was in editors' mind for a long time, I have come to understand that the eager young mind of today, will be a great historian of tomorrow for sure.

The approach of presenting this paper in the book was found to be convenient and handy. Needless to say, these all are out of context and potent for pitfalls for an independent critique and assessment. The aim of this book is to present the basic and most important topics that have not been touched by the historians so far relating to Ancient, Medieval and Modern Histories of India and Europe. This book is what the title presents itself to be and nothing else. This book is collection of various essays, which may also be referred to a greater extent as both primary as well as secondary materials for the researchers and readers.

The present collection is limited to be the basic and important aspects of the history to understand the discourse of the history learning. An attempt has also been made to discuss the untouched portion of the history ranging from ancient to modern history. The contributors, who are leading authorities in their respective fields of specialization, readily agreed and sent in their contribution. They have placed us under a deep debt of gratitude. It may, however, be stated that the views expressed by them are their own.

It is my bounden duty to record my grateful thanks to the editors, who entrusted the tasking of writing Foreword for this volume, as also to the scholars who have contributed chapters to the book.

Prabira Sethy

Prabira Sethy
Assistant Professor
Department of Pol. Science
Maharaja Agrasen College
University of Delhi
New Delhi - 110096

Preface

Every book has its own story to tell its audiences about a certain field of study. Each and every piece of writing is related to the expansion of knowledge in general. This book or we can say a collection of various research papers is not an exception to it. This book is a concoction of chapters or individual work of various authors dealing with an overview and latest developments in the field of historical research as a whole. Not only simple write-ups have been included in this volume but these altogether will try to enlighten its readers or the audiences with the ongoing research works that have been going on in historical studies.

The book will surely be a guiding light for those who want deep study of historical research. As a book of various articles related to history and culture, it will try to put forward some of the greatest developments in the concerned field. The papers presented in this volume are undoubtedly some of the important and valuable writings of our rich culture and heritage and these will profoundly affect the masses who are vigorously connected with the concerned field of research and development.

This book provides students, researchers, readers and scholars with a base, incite them to pursue further readings depending on their needs and interests. We hope that this book will communicate all the necessary details irrespective of any caste, creed, religion and gender. We would like to dedicate this book to our well-wishers.

Acknowledgement

Every piece of work in literary or any other field can be regarded as the final product of the united efforts of various personalities who actually work restlessly. Every book is undoubtedly carved out from the undying efforts of certain individuals. This book can similarly be regarded as the final version of certain restless efforts of distinct persons.

First and foremost, we thank our parents for standing beside us throughout our career and writing this book. This book is dedicated to our parents. We feel much beholden to each and every individual author of the book whose papers have been published under the banner of this book. Without them the publication of such work would not have been possible. Finally, we owe deep sense of admiration & offer our deep gratitude towards for Prabira Sethy, who has helped us throughout this journey so far.

We are in great debt to professors, research assistants and research associates of Maharaja Agrasen College for contributions as well as for their continuous support. We also extend much appreciation to our professors, teachers, relatives and friends for providing valuable feedbacks and suggestions.

We are in great depth to our publication house, Vij Books India Pvt. Ltd. for publishing our work in the definite time decided by us. We would like to acknowledge with gratitude, the support and love our families and friends who kept us going and this book would not have been possible without them. Last and not least, we beg forgiveness of all those who have been with us over the course of the years and whose names we have failed to mention.

Introduction

This book is a distillation of different ideas and views of different individuals. The book will undoubtedly serve its audiences with the appropriate information regarding the research and development in historical studies. History as a subject, as we all know, serve every human being with the definite and accurate ideas and issues related to historical events. The historical events are very much necessary to understand our present society and this book will, for sure, help the masses in various ways to understand their past better and more distinctively. Different parts of the book are meant to be used to understand a particular area or an idea. We have tried to include the various issues and events that have a great impact on our present human civilization.

This book brings into perspective the various themes that are crucial for both Indian and World History. The book comprises of three different areas of research in historical studies. The book itself reflects the historical research from the beginning of human civilization till the end of colonialism and so on. The first and most important theme is "Ancient History". Ancient or the "Old Part" which mainly revolve around the beginning of human civilization on earth and how they evolved with the passing time. Within this theme, the very first chapter titled *"Climatic Change in the Pre and Proto Historical Period: An Emphasis on the Natural Factors"* direct that changes in the climatic condition was nurtured mainly by the internal/natural factors instead of the external/human activities. However it can be stipulated that internal factors played a major role in transforming the environmental condition and this further facilitated the human to take advantage of such changes in the climate in the form of rainfall, dense vegetation and forests.

Within this theme the second chapter *"Beginning of Iron Age in India and its Extension"*, reflects author's interrogation on the beginning of the Iron Age in India. It can be seen through the discussion in the article that profound changes could be seen after the invention of iron. There was a significant development in the field of agriculture or production process which ultimately gave a huge boost to the economy in turn led to the significant changes in material culture. The chapter mainly shows the development of Iron Age culture and its significant contribution towards the development of the social set up of different regions in India during that period.

The book then tend to introduce a new set of research work titled *"Buddhism: It's Emergence & Popularity in Early India"*, dealt with the ideas and reasons behind the emergence of Buddhism as a religion and here authors scrutinize on the emergence and development of Buddhism in India during the early times. The traditional Vedic religious ideas began to vanish slowly which led to the emergence of various popular religious pantheons which comparatively began to propagate more logical ways for the attainment of salvation or *'Moksha'*. Buddhism was one of these popular cultures. The chapter further demonstrates how Buddhist ideas became widespread within a very short span of time and assumed a pan Indian character.

Our understanding for the emergence & popularity of Buddhism is more or less clear from the previous chapter. The next chapter titled *"Buddhist Theory of Kingship in Dīgha Nikāya"* focuses on the Buddhist ideology, political ideas contained in the *Dīgha Nikāya*, essential qualities & duties of a good king / ideal king. The author also emphasizes on the seven symbols of sovereignty and also analyses 'Buddha' is not a name but a 'Title' which means 'a person who is awake'. Meanwhile, author also gives brief Buddhist accounts of the origin of the state or kingship which is closely linked with its account of the evolution of the universe. Author also highlights that, according to Dīgha Nikāya, an important Buddhist account that talks of the appearance of high-quality rice and its consumption, men acquire physical strength.

Next chapter within this theme is *"The Problem of Dīdārgañj Caurī Bearer's Identification – A Response"*, in which the author emphasizes on the problems pertaining to the identification of *Dīdārgañj Caurī*, how the sculptures of Patnā and *Dīdārgañj Caurī* Bearers Compared and later on the issues with their identification. However, the last and the final chapter of this theme deals with *"Gender Depiction in Visual Art"*, here author accentuates on representation of the female body is at the center of feminist cultural politics and women artists are using images of the female body in order to make visible a range of female identities. For feminists to reclaim the female body means to challenge the authority of patriarchal boundaries - boundaries of gender and identity and between art and obscenity. It is an ongoing struggle, but with the increasing role of media and growth of a wider audience there will be more spaces opening out for feminist voices to be heard and for female images to be seen.

Second theme "Medieval History" is related with the beginning of expansion of Mohammedan faith all around the world. It shows the emergence of various Muslim invaders and how they expanded their control over certain parts of the world. The Muslim expansion can be seen profoundly in Indian subcontinent as well. Their rule to a greater extent shows the fall of the traditional Hindu customs and traditions. The first chapter of this theme titled *"The Interconnection between History and Literature"*. In this chapter, the author talks on the practice of history writing where he strongly argues that practice of history writing doesn't take place in isolation. It gets influenced by the material culture in which it is written. Thus, one can't deny the relation between history and culture. The evaluation of the nature and function of the process of history writing allow us to look into the cultural, social as well as political sphere of that period. As far as "culture" is concerned there is hardly any disapproval that literature forms an integral part of culture. Popular experiences are generally expressed through the medium of literature. Literature is able to penetrate in those areas where the modern discipline of history writing based on European principles, generally can't.

After examining the basic ideas of history writing and early civilization, in the next chapter *"Understanding the Rise of Mongol Military Power and its Implications on Research"*, author examines in detail the nature of the Mongol military machine, which would underlie the constitution of the world's second largest historical empire. The paper engages with the popular misconceptions about Mongol society and history, both on its own terms, and also in terms of comparison to other major world empires. Through examining these issues, in particular the military organization of Mongol society and also of gender and rule, the article builds notes about the implication of research on the Mongol Empire, especially in the context of its role and character in global and world empire histories.

The last chapter within the second theme is *"Historical Consciousness in Pre Modern India"*, deals with the very basic idea of treating history as a scientific, rational and objective discipline in a modern construct. Author question whether historical consciousness existed in pre modern India before the arrival of British and the modern concept of rational and scientific discipline that can be traced back to the 19th Century Europe where it is seen as a medium to explore "past realities" on the basis of verifiable evidence, studied objectively. Also, by examining various pre modern text, historical text written in different literary genre one could get a more nuanced understanding of India's rich history writing tradition which existed even before the colonial period.

The third and the final theme "Modern History" talks of an era which was full of historical research and was basically based on the invention and expansion of scientific revolution, renaissance, colonialism, capitalism, nationalism, revolts and movements, formation of new political parties and leaders, political interventions etc. which undoubtedly changed the scenario of existing human civilization. It shows how the various inventions in scientific research and other revolutionary activities shaped the world into a more advanced place. This theme begins with the chapter "*The Influence of Ancient Rome on the French Revolution and its Potential for Class Analysis*", here the author examines the influence of symbols, ideas and concepts of Ancient Rome on the French Revolution. It highlights not only the importance of such concepts on the French Revolutionaries but also the Ancient Régime of France. The article argues that, given these influences, historical analysis of Class in the French Revolution, should draw on the models of class structure of Ancient Rome itself for the purposes of evolving a coherent image of society in both Pre-and Post-Revolution France.

The second chapter titled "*Development of Indian Archaeology till the Close of the 19th Century*", the author mainly focuses on the development of Archaeological study in India. The development of archaeological research and studies related to it as a whole opened the doors to the discovery of many antiquities which can undoubtedly be regarded as the main pillars of our civilization and cultural heritage. However, it should be mentioned here that the development of archaeological studies and research in India is a gift of the European powers because the advent of the Europeans actually started the research of archaeological background of Indian subcontinent.

After discussing the development of archaeology next chapter titled "*Archaeology and Museums: Rethinking Sense of Identity in India*", deals with how a nation views its past and the significance it attaches to its heritage resembles the self-respect and identity of that nation. The past of a nation and its people is, therefore, glorified through the presence of available records, written and material. Written records are, however, susceptible to subjectivity and that makes the material remains even more crucial to studying past in entirety. The documentation of the material remains and their visuals, providing necessary breakthroughs, are preserved in museums making them part of an archaeological practice. The museums further help in shaping identity at various levels of society, viz. national, regional, local and individual.

The last and the final chapter of this text deals with "*Journey towards Modern India: Indira Priyadarshini Gandhi the Creator of New India*", the title of this chapter is more deceiving and clear. At this juncture, the author highlights the contribution of Indira Gandhi to the making of New India, Indira as a personality of being persistent with her policies and challenges as a political leader and policy maker. Indira Priyadarshini Gandhi was not only successful in her political and social career but also was successful in delivering a self-sufficient, self-reliant and stable India. We can say that Gandhi's achievements were once the backbone to the Indian nation and even it is felt that we are still continuing with some of her amendments even today.

Section — I
Ancient History

CHAPTER - ONE

Climatic Changes in the Pre and Proto Historical Periods: An Emphasis on the Natural Factors

Ashu J

This paper is not a full-fledged article in the sense it represents. But this paper represents some of the ideas pertaining to the pre and proto historical periods which precisely emphasise on the natural factors on how the climatic changes affect the human civilization. This paper gives a general introduction on how there was a steep climatic change over a decade and what was the role of human in changing the climatic condition and moreover on how these changes facilitated humans to establish its genesis.

Transition from the colder to the warmer climate had remained an issue for many centuries. It has been put forward by several environmental historians that the main factor for the increase in the temperature is due to the population and human activities. The prime objective of this research paper is to focus on changes in the climatic condition from Lower Palaeolithic of the Pleistocene Epoch to the beginning of the civilization by emphasizing that the rise in temperature was due to the natural factors rather that the human intervention.

It is clearly known that Pleistocene Epoch was the longest period of the earth and was described as the "Great Ice Age". But today only 10% of the ice covers are left and these are found mainly in Antarctica, Greenland, Iceland and mountain ranges. I emphasize mainly on the natural factor as the main precursor of these changes. The main causes for the climatic changes and glaciations are solar isolation, carbon dioxide and tectonic movements. However, we can't completely rule out the importance of the carbon dioxide for the creation of the glaciers. The level of carbon dioxide first resulted in warmer and then colder climates. In order to explain this phenomena, we should know that the solar radiations have medium and long wavelengths. Medium enters the earth's atmosphere while the long is reflected back and used to get absorbed by carbon dioxide and water vapour, producing heat up and warm atmosphere. This further enhances evaporation and thus provides moisture for additional clouds and glacier-forming precipitate. If carbon dioxide is one of the factors for the creation of the glaciers than how can we blame the increase in carbon dioxide led to rise in temperature?

Nevertheless, it is evident from the prehistoric period that it was natural forces which was moulding the environment rather the human activities. For instance, living in the naturally available shelters also submit that the human during that time was looking for caves and rock shelters in order protect themselves from severe cold which was further transformed into mud and brick houses. Also hunting of animals during the Palaeolithic period suggests that the availability of plants were hindered by the snow and colder climate. We also find numerous references of fishing activity which specifies that the environment was comparatively colder and formed the staple diet of the pre and proto historical man. On the other hand, domestication of fire between 200,000 years ago also confirms that it was first used for warming themselves instead of cooking during the initial stages. Even the domestication of animals was first started before the advent of agriculture in c. 7000-6000 BC from Mesolithic, this ultimately indicate climatic condition. Domesticate of animals such as cattle and deer, suggest that the man wanted to use the by-products of the animals as a food supplements due to the lack of vegetation and even these animals were used by them as a helper while hunter and gathering. This lack of vegetation indicates the non-availability of suitable climatic conditions for germination of edible plants. Even the study of the pollens can help us in determining the sorts of animals existing at that time and about their tolerance limit of these plants give clues as to the climate. Development of food procurement was made by man, the stress may be traced to the environment. All these illustrate the colder climatic condition during the Lower and Middle Palaeolithic period.

Lower Palaeolithic period was largely covered with ice-age on contrast the Upper Palaeolithic marked less humid and climate was comparatively warmer. Climatic changes brought about the changes in fauna and flora. I strongly believe in the internal factors such as volcanic eruption, tectonic movement, solar isolation and rotation of the earth have the main precursor of these changes rather than external factors like population and pollution. Because it is very evident that during that period the population was not too much to be considered as one of the major factor for the change in climatic conditions. Looking into the technological factors the technology such as the tools and other objects made and used by the pre and proto historical man was naturally made and it is impossible to think that it has ever made a worse impact on environment. It can be said that earth was eventually transforming itself in order to maintain a balance between flora and fauna. We can't forget that ice of Pleistocene glaciers originally came from the oceans which involved first the formation of evaporation than winds followed by snow and ice. However, isostasy (condition of balance) helps us in understanding the ice-sheet areas and other changes that had brought about.

We should note that rainfall certainly helped human society during the pre and proto historic periods in pursuing agriculture. The coming of the rainfall after the post-glacier era doesn't take place in vacuum. It is very easy to understand this transition, rivers were formed from the melting of the ice due to the increase in the temperature by heat of the sun or any other natural factors like volcanic eruption, change in the temperature of the earth's core, etc. and further resulting in evaporation process followed by formation of clouds and finally by rain. This can be looked upon as: -

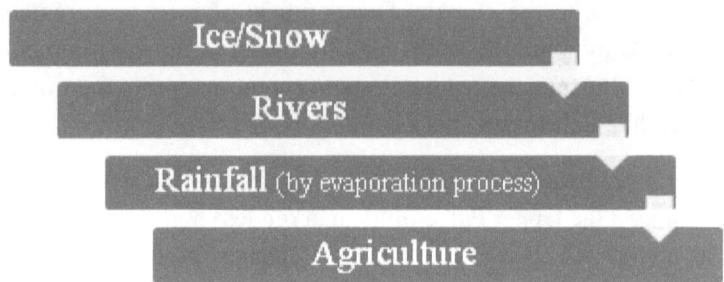

To conclude it can be pronounced that change in the climatic condition was nurtured mainly by the internal/natural factors instead of the external/human activities. However it can be stipulated that internal factors played a major role in the transforming the environmental condition and this further facilitated the human to take advantage of such change in the climate in the form of rainfall, dense vegetation and forests. We should not always rely on the human intervention as the main agent for the climatic changes during the pre and proto historical period. The environment has a direct bearing on human efforts. Although it is true that human efforts substantially affect the natural surroundings but not to that extend during the particular period.

References

Bhattacharya, D.K. (1986). Ecology and Social Formation in Ancient History. Delhi: Sandeep Prakashan.

Eicher, Don L. and A. Lee McAlester (1980). History of the Earth. USA: Englewood Cliffs Prentice Hall.

Jain, V.K. (2009). Prehistory and Protohistory of India: An Appraisal – Palaeolithic – Non-Harappan Chalcolithic Cultures. New Delhi: D.K. Printworld (P) Ltd.

Quante, Markus (2010). Relict Species: Phylogeography and Conservation Biology. Germany: Springer Berlin Heidelberg.

Sharma, R.S. (2005). India's Ancient Past. New Delhi: Oxford University Press.

CHAPTER - TWO

Beginning of Iron Age in India and its Extension

Srotoswini Borah

By the end of the Chalcolithic period, the rural settlements had come up in all parts of India. However, the major changes in the material culture were brought about with the use of iron. In archaeology generally the Iron Age is defined as the stage in the development of any human civilization in which iron was used as the main ingredient for making tools and weapons. If we look at the world context, the advent of the Iron Age in Mesopotamia is dated around 1300 B.C. The earliest evidences of iron objects can be found in the Egyptian graves of 3000 B.C. It is also important to mention here that the Anatolian (Turkish Empire) people used iron from about 3rd millennium B.C. to 1200 B.C.

Regarding India, the earlier evidences of the Iron Age can be found in the North-western and Southern Indian regions. This is regarded as the earliest stage. The second stage expansion can be seen in the Upper Gangetic region. This stage's development in the iron technology is popularly tagged as the mature period which expanded from 1000 to 800 B.C.E. The late phase or the last phase can be seen from about 800 to 600 B.C.E. This period is associated with the Black on Red Ware (B.R.W) culture, which is the earliest phase of the Northern Black Polished Ware (N.B.P.W) culture.

The earliest evidences of the use of iron in India can be traced both from archaeological and literary evidences. For example, if we look at the Gandhar grave region in the North-western India then much kind of iron objects can be seen discovered along with the dead bodies in the graves. Besides, the Upper Gangetic region consisted of places like Kausambi and Ahichchatra has yielded various specimens of iron objects. The iron specimens have also been recovered from the Malwa region during the later Chalcolithic period. The Megalithic burial sites of the Southern Indian region and the Deccan regions of the Chalcolithic period also yielded various iron objects.

Iron Age in India has been broadly divided into three sub-categories or sub-periods consisting of the 1st period which expanded from 1200 to 1000 B.C.E. over the region of Pirak and Hallur of Baluchistan and Karnataka in India respectively. The 2nd period consisted of the extension in the Gangetic region from 1000 to 800 B.C.E. The last period expanded from 800 to 600 B.C.E.

Various archaeological evidences show the expansion of iron culture in the Indian subcontinent. For example, copper objects containing iron ores have been found in the places like Lothal in Gujarat of the Harappan civilization. But it is to be mentioned here that these objects were really copper objects with some iron ores according to some scholars. In reality iron was not familiar to Harappans at all.

If we look at the Megalithic culture of Southern Indian region and Deccan, the earliest evidences of iron objects can be found in the overlapping period of Neolithic and Megalithic phases. Some scholars try to conclude that the Megalithic culture in South India was a full-fledged Iron Age culture when the great benefits of the use of iron began to be realized by the people. Most of the information regarding this Iron Age in Southern India can be gathered from the excavations of the various Megalithic burials. Almost in every Megalithic burial, iron objects have been found extending from the region of Junapani near Nagpur in Vidarbha of central India down to Adichchanallur in Tamilnadu in far South. Thirty three types of iron tools have been recovered from various regions of the Indian subcontinent ranging from celt, axe, chisel, adze, knife, fish hook, arrow, trident, etc.

Iron production was not easy as copper working since the metal obtained had to be reheated and go through several critical processes and then hammered continuously for making it useful. Moreover, it did not melt at the same temperature as that of smelting copper. Mass production of copper/bronze objects was possible through casting in a single smelt. However, iron needed extensive man-hours to forge them and make functional artifacts. Though these difficulties were present, but iron was adopted due to its strength. Tools made of it were more efficient for working in comparison to the bronze ones. Therefore, it was quickly adopted and spread in a very short span of time after its initial appearance. Ropar and Hastinapur in the Upper Gangetic valley have not yielded any iron objects due to which many scholars suggest that this phase belonged to pre-Iron Age culture though these two are PGW culture sites. But iron was found at a later stage in these two sites.

In South India, one can trace the earliest Iron Age sites. It includes places like Hallur, Karnataka and Adichchanallur in Tamil Nadu. There is evidence of iron at Pirak belonging to 1000 B.C. and in the graves of Gandhara of 1000 B.C. At Jakhera in Upper Ganga Valley, iron implements have been found. Atranjikhera in Uttar Pradesh has also yielded iron implements like tongs, spearheads, axes, knives, etc. In the Deccan, 1st iron objects appear after the late Jorwe Chalcolithic phase extending from 900-800 B.C.E.

Regarding literary evidences, many works have mentioned about the existence of iron through various ways. For example, there is mention of a term *'Ayas'* in the *Rig Veda* which is taken as iron by many scholars. But according to various scholars, the term *'Ayas'* means either sharpness or strength or may be both. Besides, the various texts of the Later Vedic period, however, clearly mention about iron by the name 'Shyam' or 'Krishna' Ayas which means black or dark metal. This black metal undoubtedly identified as iron by the prominent scholars. Besides, Yajurveda and Atharvaveda clearly mention about iron which is used in the agricultural activities. *Taittiriya Samhita* of the *Yajurveda* mentions about Ayas and at least there is one reference to smiths. The *Atharvaveda* mentions about an amulet born of a ploughshare smitten away with a knife by a skillful smith. The other texts like the *Śatapatha Brāhmaṇa* connects ion with peasantry. Again, the early Buddhist texts like the *Sutta Nipata* mentions about various objects made of iron. The term *'Ayovikara'* in the *Ashtadhyayi* of Panini has been translated as iron ploughshare.

Different types of iron tools connected with different works have been identified ranging from the early to late Iron Age. These iron tools are identified as to be connected with various functions ranging from agriculture to hunting and household to building and craft tools. Agricultural tools consisting of the axes, sickle, ploughshare, hoe, spearhead, arrowhead, points, blades, daggers, swords, elephant goads, etc. were used for hunting. In household works various iron tools like knife, disc, ring, spoon, etc. were used. For building or construction purposes, rod, pin, nail, pipe, socket, chain, door hook, etc. were used. These various kinds of tool in reality show the development of iron technology in almost every nook and corner of the Indian subcontinent.

However, it is important to mention here that the iron technology in India brought a tremendous change in the socio, political and economic arenas. Regarding economy, iron brought a significance change in the agriculture. Agricultural process became advanced due to use of sophisticated iron implements which not only decreased the labour in the fields but also gave a tremendous increment in the agricultural production. Due to the advancement in the agricultural economy, surplus production began to happen and with this trade and commerce began to flourish which ultimately resulted in the establishment of various urban centers. In the Ganga valley and Malwa region iron led to the rise of urban areas. Later *Vedic* and *Brahminical* texts mention vigorously about the newly emerging urban cities in these regions. 16 *Mahajanapadas* are the examples of these kinds of emerging political centers. Some of the urban centers were also seats of political power. Thus, a political system with territorial units as their bases had developed by this time. The expansion of cities and trade led to the introduction or perhaps re-introduction of writing into ancient India.

In religious sphere, consequently some significant changes can be noticed. The traditional *Vedic* religion was a communal one, well adapted to small-scale tribal societies. But with the growth of various independent states and the growing number of merchants, nobles and urban people began looking for a more personal religious experience, one which would speak to their individual need for salvation. Moreover, the high importance and value given to Priests under the *Vedic* pantheon created a situation unacceptable for the common people and ultimately led to the emergence of new creeds like Buddhism and Jainism.

So, it can be seen there was profound development of the socio-economic conditions of ancient India during the later *Vedic* period with the emergence of Iron Age. The overall development of the Indian subcontinent prepared the way for the greater advancement of every aspect of the society, economy and polity.

References

Banerjee, N.R. (1964). The Iron Age in India. New Delhi: Munshiram Manoharial.

Jain, V.K. (2009). Prehistory and Protohistory of India: An Appraisal – Palaeolithic – Non-Harappan Chalcolithic Cultures. New Delhi: D.K. Printworld (P) Ltd.

Maiti, P. (1964). Studies in Ancient India. Kolkata: Shreedhar Prakashani.

CHAPTER - THREE

Buddhism: It's Emergence & Popularity in Early India

Bitumani Tahbildar & Srotoswini Borah

Background

In the 6th century B.C. there was a decline in the authority of old *Vedic* religion. The first reason for this change is that the *Upanisads* had introduced a spirit of enquiry about the fundamental problems of life, in the light of which much of the *Vedic* ideas appeared unsatisfactory. Due to the prevalence of the four *Ashramas*, many people adopted the last two *Ashramas* i.e. *Banaprastha* and *Sannyasa* and began to live the life of ascetics. Many of them were non-Brahmins and *Kshatriyas*. They pointed out that *Yajna* and worship cannot release a man from the law of the deed done (*Karmafalas*). They denied the efficacy of the Vedic form of worship and the supremacy of the *Brahmanas*. They advocated the doctrine of Right Conduct as the only means that could liberate the 'Soul' from *Karmafala*. The people directed their enquiry to the fundamental problems of life and the ideas preached by them highly transformed the old *Brahminical* beliefs. Romila Thaper has pointed out that the "social and economic changes such as the growth of the towns, expansion of the artisan class and the rapid development of trade and commerce were linked with the change in religion and philosophical speculation."

The *Vedic* or *Brahminical* form of worship was began to be regarded as burdensome by the non-Brahmin parts of the social system. The poorer classes began to criticize these rituals due to which slowly the *Brahminical* religion lost its attraction among the poorer classes.

The protest against the *Vedic* religion led to the emergence of a number of new religious creeds viz. Buddhism, Jainism, *Ajivikism* and devotional creeds like *Bhagvatism* and *Saivism*. During the 6th century B.C. mounting arose against the prevailing of the *Brahminical* religion. The *Ajivika* creed became popular at this time. Its preacher Gosala Mankhaliputta was a fundamental thinker who challenged the basic tenets of *Brahminical* religion. Ultimately, Buddhism superseded *Ajivikism*, because the latter was too pessimistic and negative in approach. It failed to present an alternative creed for which ultimately Buddhism succeeded in establishing its firm footing on the Indian subcontinent as a dominant religious creed.

Origin & the Early Development of the Creed

The origin of Buddhism points to one man, Siddhartha Gautama, the historical Buddha, who was born in Lumbini (presently Nepal) during the 5th century BCE. Rather than the founder of a new religion, Siddhartha Gautama was the founder and leader of a sect of wanderer ascetics (*Sramanas*), one of many sects that existed at that time all over India.

The *Sramanas* movement which originated in the culture of world renunciation that emerged in India from about the 7th century BCE, was the common origin of many religious and philosophical traditions in India, including the *Charvaka* School, Buddhism, and its sister religion, Jainism. The *Sramanas* rejected the *Vedic* teachings, which was the traditional religious order in India, and renounced conventional society.

Siddharth Gautama lived during a time of profound social changes in India. The authority of the *Vedic* religion was being challenged by a number of new religious and philosophical views. This religion had been developed by a nomadic society roughly a millennium before Siddhartha's time and it gradually gained hegemony over most of North India, especially in the Gangetic Plain. But things were different in the 5th century BCE as society was no longer nomadic because agrarian settlements had replaced the old nomad caravans and evolved into villages, then into towns and finally into cities. Under the new urban context, a considerable sector of Indian society was no longer satisfied with the old *Vedic* faith.

After Siddhartha Gautama passed away, the community he founded slowly evolved into a religion-like movement and the teachings of Siddhartha became the basis of Buddhism. The historical evidence suggests that Buddhism had a humble beginning. Apparently, it was a relatively minor tradition in India, and some scholars have proposed that the impact of the Buddha in his own days was limited due to the scarcity of written documents, inscriptions and archaeological evidence from that time.

By the 3rd century BCE, the picture we have of Buddhism is very different. The Mauryan Indian emperor Ashoka, the Great (304-232 BCE), turned Buddhism into the state religion of India. He provided a favourable social and political climate for the acceptance of Buddhist ideas, encouraged Buddhist missionary activity, and even generated among Buddhist monks certain expectations of patronage and influence on the machinery of political decision making. Archaeological evidence for Buddhism between the death of the Buddha and the time of Ashoka is scarce; after the time of Ashoka it is abundant.

Fundamental Principles of Buddhism or Dhamma

The earliest available source of our knowledge for Buddha's teachings (*Dhamma*) is the Pali 'Pitakas' and 'Nikāyas'. The Pitakas consist of three parts, the *Vinaya*, the *Sutta* and the *Avidhamma*. The '*Sutta Pitaka*' is the most important source for the study of Buddha's teachings. It is divided into 5 Nikāyas.

The '*Avidhamma Pitaka*' contains the philosophical aspects of Buddhism. In any case the doctrines laid down in the *Sutras* suffered additions and alterations in the hands of Buddha's many disciples in later years. So what we get from the Sutras today may not be in totality original teachings of Buddha.

Buddha instructed his followers to observe practical methods to arrive at the Truth, to attain happiness and to overcome sufferings. He asked his disciples to comprehend the Four Noble Truths (*Aryasatyani*), viz. a) that there is sorrow and suffering; this suffering is due to existence in this World. Man suffers from disease, old age and non-fulfillment of desire due to existence in this world. b) There are causes of suffering like desire, attachment which lead to worldly existence. c) The suffering can be ended by the destruction of desire. d) There is a way (*Marga* or *Path*) for the destruction of desire leading to suffering.

D. D. Kausambi has tried to give a social explanation of the Four Truths. Every man seeks to overcome his sorrow and suffering and seeks for happiness. Those who are violent or crude by nature seek to be happy by injuring the interests of others. But Buddha pointed out an entirely new 'path' for deliverance from suffering. He said that desire is the root cause of sorrow and suffering. To overcome desire is to overcome suffering.

After explaining the chain of causes that lead to suffering, Buddha outlined the 'Eightfold Paths' (*Astangika Marga*) for deliverance from suffering. These 'Eightfold Paths' were as follows- 1) Right Speech, 2) Right action, 3) Right means of livelihood, 4) Right Exertion, 5) Right mindedness, 6) Right meditation, 7) Right resolution and 8) Right point of view. The practice of the first three principles would lead to the attainment of physical control or *Sila*. The next three would lead to the attainment of mental control or *Samadhi* and the practice of the last two principles would lead to the development of insight or *Prajna*.

Buddha said that one can escape from suffering and sorrow only when he attains the *'Nirvana'*. Buddha did not mention the existence of God, nor did he mention the *Vedas*. Though he did not openly deny the caste system, he did not accept it either. He said that anybody, belonging to any caste whatsoever could escape from misery and suffering by observing the 'Eight-fold Path'. According to the *'Sutta Nipata'* Buddha said, "One doesn't become a Brahmin by birth. One doesn't become an outcast by birth. One becomes a Brahmin by act. One becomes an outcast by act." Buddha advised his disciples, that those who will follow the 'Eight-fold Path' and *'Majjhima Pantha'* or Middle Path strictly, will be strong in spirit and mind. He will be able to enter any society with confidence, self-dignity. He will die without desire and anxiety.

Buddha's moral codes were free from cast restrictions and complicated form of worship for which they attracted the low castes and *Sudras* to his fold. Buddha didn't accept the supremacy of the Brahmins and their claim to divinity. He even ascribed the term *'Kulaputtas'* or noble *Kula* or birth to *Gahapatis* and rich merchants. His religion also satisfied the *Kshatriya* caste who were jealous of the Brahmins.

Thus Buddhism tried to break the social barrier erected by the Brahmins. He provided the common men and alternative way of salvation and solace. His doctrine of non-violence found in the *Sutta Nipata* tried to promote social harmony. Non killing of animals help the protection of cow, which provided milk to the old and infant, and the bullocks which were so essential for drawing the plough. Buddha didn't only preach social harmony, he also advocated the upliftment of women. He prescribed five principles of good behavior. People were asked to abstain from: 1. Killing, 2. Taking what is not given to want, 3. Adultery, 4. False Hood and 5. Indolence.

Buddha didn't neglect the womankind. The Brahminical laws sought to deprive them of their rights, reduced them to state of virtual slavery. Buddha preached their liberation. He recognized their right of doing all types of work suitable for them and asked them to defy '*Purdah*'. He started the order of Nuns or *Bhikshuni Samgha* permitted the women to join it. He had even a sympathetic heart for the prostitutes who according to him were victims of circumstances. Buddha laid down seven rules for the republic of Vriji and the fifth rule was that people of Vriji must treat the women with honour. No woman, either married or unmarried should be oppressed. Buddha preached his sermons in *Ardha-Magadhi* language which was the spoken dialect of the people so that his message could reach the poor and underdogs of the society.

Buddhist Philosophy and Its Influence

Buddhism can be regarded as a body of moral principles rather than a metaphysical system. But in course of time philosophical background became necessary for its survival and propagation. Dr. S. Radhakrishnan has pointed out that Buddhism and Brahmanism form a single system of philosophy.

The Buddhist philosophy had its main root in doctrine of *Karma* (Law of the Deed done). The *Upanishadic* theory of *Karma*, that the effect of deeds regulates future births was accepted by Buddha. He therefore, concluded that since results of *Karma* or deeds affect future birth, good deeds would lead to higher birth leading to ultimate salvation of the soul. But Buddha never clearly expressed his views on the soul or the beginning and end of this world. Buddha shared the prevailing pessimism of the time and regarded life and worldly existence as a source of misery. Therefore, he advocated the theory that true happiness can come if one can get his deliverance from rebirth. Thus, in his belief in the doctrine of *Karma* and in his advocacy for deliverance from rebirth, Buddha was influenced by *Upanishadic* ideas.

Buddhism is supposed to have been much influenced by the *Sankhya* philosophy and the older system of yoga and *dhyana*. Buddha rejected the Brahminical doctrine of *Yajna* and Good deed as path to salvation. The Buddhist *Suttas* contain the theory that one can attain the *Brahma Loka* by performing Good deeds, but the soul can't be liberated from rebirth by that.

Early Buddhism as such looked upon salvation of the individual as the goal. But it faced criticism from Brahminical thinkers that Brahminical philosophy preached salvation of all beings but Buddhism pursued a narrow aim by preaching only salvation of the man. Buddhism underwent some transformations due to this criticism. The orthodox Buddhists who stuck to the original view of the salvation of the individual came to be known as *Hinayanists* (having a lower aim) and who preached salvation of all beings as their aim, came to be known as *Mahayanists*. The second i.e., the *Mahayana* system bore the influence of Brahminical philosophy to a greater extent than the *Hinayana* creed.

Buddha rejected the authority of the *Vedas* and condemned animal sacrifices. The Brahminical Gods and the concept of Heaven (*Svarga*) were rejected by him. Buddha's teachings were ethical and rational. It was based on the concept of equality of man. He rejected the doctrine of caste. He said that anyone can attain salvation by practicing the Eightfold principles. He propagated the doctrine of *Ahimsa* or Non-violence. Animal sacrifices in the *Yajna* was deplored by him.

Buddhism as a system of release from earthly suffering was anticipated by various other sects. The Buddhists had their forerunner in the *Nirganthas*, the *Ajivakas* and others. They all aimed at salvation of the soul in order to get rid of suffering of the world. The man who strove for peace was called the *Sramana* or the Toiler. The Sramana ideal existed before the rise of Buddhism. Subsequently Buddha adopted it and added more attributes to the ideal.

Progress of Buddhism

Buddhism came as a great relief to the society, ridden with

Brahminical priests and castes. The deep humanism in Buddhism and its freedom from ceremonials and its upholding of equality of man made a tremendous impact on the people. Its anti-caste preaching drew the underdogs of the society under its banner. Buddhism increased their faith in their own existence and led to the growth of their self-confidence. Even in the lifetime of Buddha i.e., in the 6th century B.C., Magadha, Kosala, Kausambhi and the tribal republics of the Sakyas, Vrijis, Mallas, etc. were swept by Buddhism. After the death of the Great Lord, his self-less disciples and the Buddhist *Samgha* carried the evangelical work with great vigour. Bimbisara, Aajatasatru and many other famous rulers embraced Buddhism. Asoka was the Constantine of Buddhism. The patronage given by Asoka to this creed converted Buddhism from a local sect to a world religion. Asoka declared it as a state religion and took various measures to preach his *Dhamma* both in and outside India. After the death of Asoka, Buddhism received a great patronage from Kanishka under whom Buddhism entered Central Asia and China. Thus, a local sect of the Gangetic valley turned to be a world religion.

Fracture of Buddhism and Emergence of the Different Buddhist Schools

There are many stories about disagreements among the disciples of Buddha which ultimately led to the emergence of different Buddhist schools. There are also accounts about disputes among the followers of Buddha during the First Buddhist Council held soon after the Buddha's death, suggesting that dissent was present in the Buddhist community from an early stage. After the death of the Buddha, those who followed his teachings had formed settled communities in different locations. Language differences, doctrinal disagreements, the influence of non-Buddhist schools, loyalties to specific teachers, and the absence of a recognized overall authority or unifying organizational structure are just some examples of factors that contributed to sectarian fragmentation.

About a century after the death of Buddha, we find the first major schism ever recorded in Buddhism- the *Mahasanghika* School. Many different schools of Buddhism had developed at that time. Buddhist tradition speaks about 18 schools of early Buddhism, although we know that there were more than that, probably around 25. A Buddhist school named *Sthaviravada* was the most powerful of the early schools of Buddhism. Traditionally, it is held that the *Mahasanghika* School came into existence as a result of a dispute over monastic practice.

During the 1st century C.E., while the oldest Buddhist groups were growing in south and south-east Asia, a new Buddhist school named Mahayana (Great Vehicle) originated in northern India. This school had a more adaptable approach and was open to doctrinal innovations. Mahayana Buddhism is today the dominant form of Buddhism in Nepal, Tibet, China, Japan, Mongolia, Korea and Vietnam.

Conclusion

Buddhism had a great relevance to the society. This protestant creed arose out of a social and economic transformation in the 6th century B.C. Hence, Buddhism came as an answer to some of the growing problems in the society. The prevailing pessimism of the time which was reflected in growing disbelief in the Brahminical form of worship and sacrifices found an echo in Buddha's thought.

During the 19th and 20th centuries, Buddhism responded to new challenges and opportunities that cut across the regional religious and cultural patterns that characterized the Buddhist world in the pre-modern period. Although Buddhism is a distinct religious tradition, many people in the contemporary West have adopted philosophical and practical aspects of Buddhism and incorporated them into their religious and social practices; thus there are people who identify themselves as "Buddhist Christians", "Buddhist Jews", and "Buddhist Atheists".

References

Maiti, P. (1964). Studies in Ancient India. Kolkata: Shreedhar Prakashani.

Sharma, R.S. (2005). India's Ancient Past. Oxford: Oxford University Press.

Singh, Upinder (2009). A History of Ancient and Early Medieval India. New Delhi: Pearson Education India.

CHAPTER - FOUR

Buddhist Theory of Kingship in Agañña Sutta of Dīgha Nikāya

Prabira Sethy

Life Sketch of Siddhartha Gautama Buddha

The founder of Buddhism is called the *Buddha i.e.* the Enlightened One. It is the title of his rank, and not his own personal name (Hackmann, H. and Theol, Lic, 1910, p. 1) to whom his followers in reverence for him speak of. His personal name was Siddhartha and Gautama was his surname. Of all the religious preachers of the sixth century B.C. Gautama Buddha is the best known. Siddhartha also known Gautama was born in 563 B.C. (according to modern historical research) near Kapilavatthuin the *Kshatriya* tribe of the *Shakyas* headed by his father Suddhodhana; his mother was Mahamaya. As a young prince Gautama received the usual Kshatriya training in the art of warfare. Like Mahavira, he was married to a cousin whose name was Yasodhara, and begot a son Rahula. But smitten by the sorrows of life he left his home at the age of 29, shaved off his hair and became an ascetic. He went from place to place seeking guidance, without satisfaction. As a last resort, for the sake of salvation, he gave up asceticism and took to meditation. He preached his sermon at Sarnath near Banaras and won back five disciples who had deserted him when he had abandoned the rigid path of asceticism. This sermon was called the Turning of the Wheel of Law (*dharmachakra pravartana*) and formed the nucleus of all Buddhist teachings. For 45 years Gautama Buddha wandered on foot to propagate his ideas. But in the west he did not travel beyond Kaushambi; in the east he regularly passed through Rajgir and Gaya and also visited Dakhinagiri near Mirzapur on the southern bank of the Ganga. He made the final discovery at Gaya under a *Pipal* tree on the bank of the Niranjana river (the modern Phalgu).He died at 80 at Kushinara. His death is said to have been caused by a meal of pork (*sukaramaddava*), which he had taken with his lay disciple Chunda at Pava.

Buddha is a title, not the name of a person. Derived from root budh, "to know" it means one who knows in the sense of having become one with the highest object of knowledge, supreme Truth (Murthy, 1991, p. 31). Gautama is the historical founder of Buddhism and Buddhism is the name given to the teachings of Gautama Buddha. The political ideas contained in the *Dīgha Nikāya* can be analysed in the following headings:

What is *Dīgha Nikāya*?

Digha literally means long discourses and *Nikāya* means collection. So *Dīgha Nikāya* means the collection of long discourses and is the first section of the *Sutta Pitaka* (a collection of the religious discourses of Buddha). The *Sutta Pitaka* consists of the five "*Nikāyas*" i.e. *Digha, Majjhima, Samyutta, Anguttara, Khuddaka*. So *Dīgha Nikāya* (400-300 B.C.) is one of the five *Nikāyas*. This *Nikāya* contains a huge mass of the Buddhist canonical literature in the Pali language consisting of the collection of discourses of Lord Buddha and his sayings, songs, narratives etc. Thus *Dīgha Nikāya* is a collection of dialogues of mostly of Lord Siddhartha Gautama Buddha himself. Buddha is himself principal interlocutor in conversation with his principal disciples. *Sutta* means a thread or string (on which jewels are strung) thus applied to that part of the Pali canon containing the narratives about dialogues by the Buddha. There are 180 controversial dialogues – the first dialogue is *Brahmajala* - the perfect net. *Aggañña Sutta* is number 27 of *Dīgha Nikāya*.

What is Kingship?

Monarchy was the dominant political institution of the Buddha's time. The *Dīgha Nikāya* categorically proclaims that the king was merely the chosen leader of the people, appointed by them to restrain crime and protect life and property of the people (Appadorai, 1992, p. 2). If the first king was elected on the basis of a specific agreement, kingship is an institution had passed far beyond that stage in course of time. The power of the king rested on the possession of certain material conditions and non-material attributes. Among the material conditions one is the possession of a full treasury (*paripunnakothagara*) and another is a large, strong and well-equipped army. These two are naturally related to control over territory, the concrete basis of sovereignty. The territory of a state is variously stated as comprising the capital (*rajadhani*), towns (*nigama*), villages (*gama*), countryside (*janapada*) and border areas (*paccanta*). Over all these the king has control and the right to tax the people resident therein. It is this wealth that enabled a king to maintain his armed forces with which he was capable of meeting challenges to his own position. The army is generally described as four-fold (*caturangini*) consisting of the elephant corps, cavalry, the chariot-corps and infantry. The non-material attributes forming the basis of kingship says kingship is generally regarded as a reward for meritorious actions performed in past births. The Pali texts generally insist that a king be a *Kshatriya* and belong to a family with a hoary lineage. This is in keeping with the early Buddhist view that the *Kshatriyas* are the highest among classes and castes. Nor is a woman favoured as a ruler (Gokhale, 1994, pp. 112-113).

The kingship was endowed with mystical power or a charisma which makes obedience on the part of subjects to the ruler as a quasi-religious duty. This charisma was made manifest in a number of things associated with the king. It resides in his flag or in the conch with the spiritual turning right wise used during his coronation. It is definitely associated with the insignia of kingship such as the slippers, sword, diadem, fan, throne and the white umbrella. It is even associated with the place where he was born, the place where he was crowned and the place where he wins his most significant victory which are declared as "memorable spots" (Gokhale, 1994, p. 114).

The *Tesakuna Jataka* contains material on early Buddhist political ideas and among them is the concept of the five powers (*balani*) which are the bases of kingship. These five powers are described as strength of arms (*bahabalam*), strength of wealth (*bhogabalam*), strength of ministers (*amaccabalam*), prestige of high birth (*abhijaccabalam*), and strength of intellect (*pannabalam*), the last being the greatest of royal strengths. There is no reference to forts or fortifications being regarded as a distinct element in kingship in Buddhist literature though references to fortified capitals, towns and frontier places are fairly frequent (Gokhale, 1994, pp. 112-113).

The early Buddhist philosophy of kingship is a compound of three distinct attitudes. First, the early Buddhists betray feelings of disquiet bordering on fear about the nature and functions of kingship as it existed in their times. Second, they see no alternative to it and declare it as absolutely essential to prevent humanity lapsing into a state of anarchy. Finally, confronted with the fact of kingship and its absolute necessity for orderly human existence, they attempt to tame absolute political power by infusing into it a spirit of higher morality (Gokhale, 1994, p. 110).

The Buddha himself admits the difficulty of ruling without the use of force in any manner and under all circumstances, and the history of Buddhist kingship in India and elsewhere shows as much use of violence in internal and external relations as in other systems. Nor is it known that the Buddh advised total disarmament by a state. One measure that the Buddha took in expressing his disapproval of the institution of war was to forbid the monks from witnessing army-parades and reviews. In spite of these seeming compromises in practice, early Buddhist political thought insists on the principle of non-violence and non-injury as the ideal basis of statecraft and hopes to minimise the violence inherent in the power of the state by ordaining that this power be, at all times, restrained by morality. For the early Buddhists the world was a rational structure wherein rational laws should prevail. For them the state was not merely a punitive instrument but primarily an agency for the moral transformation of man as a political animal. They found in morality of a higher order the solution to the dilemma of power. If there is no morality there can be no state which is synonymous with order and security of life and property. In the absence of morality even the progression of the functions of nature is seriously affected for the natural order is upheld by morality. The distinct contributions of the early Buddhists to political theory in ancient India were the acceptance of a higher morality as the guiding spirit behind the state. The state was created through a demand for the rule of morality and it is this morality that stands between social order and incipient or actual anarchy. Finally, the early Buddhist argument was that morality exists for and by itself and cannot be associated with notions of ritual purity and impurity; the state must function as an instrument of this higher and universal morality for the transformation of man from being a merely political creature into a wholly moral being (Gokhale, 1994, pp. 116, 117, 118).

Buddhist View of the Origin of State or Kingship in a Social Contract

There is a great deal of canonical writings which set out the Buddhist view of the origin and the development of society and man's place in it. Among them, the *Aggañña Sutta* of the *Dīgha Nikāya* contains a complete theory of the evolution of man and his socio-political institutions. The theory as narrated in the *Aggañña Sutta* is as follows: In the early past when the world began to dissolve itself, the beings living in it began to migrate to the World of Radiance where they lived happily for a long period of time. And when the world began to re-evolve, they left it for this earth and continued to live there as human beings for a long time. The earth at that time was a mass of water and was completely dark, there being neither the sun, the moon nor the stars. Day and night and the concept of time were not known yet. There was no distinction between man and woman. All beings were reckoned simply as beings only. They were self-luminous and needed no food. They were formless and could traverse through the air. They lived exceedingly happily. On the watery earth, there emerged a layer of scum endowed with colour, odour and taste (Dissanayake, 2009, p. 7).

One day, a being of greedy disposition tasted the palatable earthly scum with its finger. Then it became suffused with the taste and craving or desire (*tanha*) was established in it. Thus, desire came to be established in the world. With the emergence of desire, self-luminance of beings faded away, followed by the manifestation of the sun and moon and starts together with day and night, and months and years. Thus, the world came into existence again. When human beings continued to feed on the scum of the earth their bodies became solid and their complexion became more comely looked down on the less comely. This resulted in conceit and pride and then the palatable earthly scum disappeared (Dissanayake, 2009, p. 7).

With this disappearance, an outgrowth in the soil like mushrooms appeared and the beings then began to feed on this. Their bodies became more solid and the difference in their comeliness more strongly marked. When the more comely beings started to despise the less comely, their conceit and pride grew stronger and the outgrowth in the soil disappeared. There appeared then the *badalata* creeper, which became the food of the beings. Owing to the change of food, their bodies became still more solid and comeliness still further marked. With the comeliness of their bodies becoming more divergent, their pride and conceit grew stronger. The *badalata* creeper then disappeared and rice appeared. The beings gathered the rice from the fields every morning and evening and as a result of feeding on rice their bodies became still more solid and human beings with distinctive male and female features appeared. Thereafter, men fell in love with women and they indulged themselves in sexual intercourse. When some people frowned on their behaviour, they built houses, began to live in them as husbands and wives, and continued to feed on the rice, which they gathered from the fields. Thus the institution of family came into existence. One day a lazy person thought that he would save the bother of going to the field every morning and evening by gathering, at one journey, sufficient rice both for breakfast and supper. Ten others followed his example and began to gather at one journey, enough rice up to eight days. Later on, the people thought that it would be convenient for every one if they divided the rice fields among themselves. They did so and set boundaries round their individual plots. So, the land which had hitherto been owned in common became privately owned. Thus arose the idea of private property in society (Dissanayake, 2009, pp. 7-8).

One day a greedy person while enjoying rice from his own plot stole rice from a plot of land belonging to another. The people admonished him against repetition of such evil conduct and he promised not to repeat it; but soon afterwards he did it again and again. The people then assaulted him with sticks and hands and censored him. This was the beginning of stealing, lying, censure and punishment. Another day the people assembled together and taking note of the growth of evil tendencies among them, recognised the need to maintain a certain moral standard among themselves. They also decided to select one among them to function as the guardian of morals, and selected the most capable, popular and handsome person among them for the post which would carry the responsibility for dispensing justice. He was required to censure and punish those who deserved such punishments and when he consented to accept the post, he was promised a share of their produce as a reward of his services. As he was elected by the whole of society, he was called *Maha Sammata* (the great elect); since he was the lord of the fields (in the sense that he had the last word in disputes relating to the rice fields) he was known as *Kshatriya* (the lord of the field); and as he pleased everyone by dispensing justice (or by the maintenance of the law or *Dhamma*), he was given the title of *Raja* (the one who pleases). Thus the idea of government originated in the world. Thereafter, some people who thought that they must give up evil tendencies which had grown among them, left their households and went to the forest to practice meditation. As they were anxious to banish (*bahenti*) evil, they were called *Brahmanas*. Some others, who wished to lead household lives, took to various (*vessa*) trades and lived with their wives and children. They came to be known as *Vessas*. The remainder took to hunting and similar rough means (*luddacara*) of livelihood and were therefore called *Suddas* or Śudras. Thus the society was stratified and the social classes came into being. This is briefly the story of the evolution of society and of the idea of Government as depicted in the *Aggañña Sutta* (Dissanayake, 2009, pp. 8-9).

Though the narration given above is not a historically accurate account of the evolution of human society, it is an attempt to interpret the evolution of man and of his social and political institutions from the Buddhist point of view. Thus, Buddhist view of the origin of the state stands the struggle for existence before the formation of the state as a manifestation of man's ignorance rather than his innate depravity. It held that man was ever ready to live in peace and amity with his fellow beings, to cooperate with them, and even to sacrifice himself for the sake of his fellow beings provided he was properly guided. Buddha argued that man could be controlled more effectively by self-understanding and inward discipline rather than by the discipline imposed from above by an external authority (Gauba, 2015, p. 34).

Essential Qualities of a Good King / Ideal King

The *Nikāyas* mention some qualities attributed to the king. It is said that a king should be well born on both sides, on the mother's side and on the father's, of pure descent back through seven generations, and neither slur nor reproach would be cast upon him in respect of birth. He should be handsome, pleasant in appearance, fair in colour, fine in presence, and stately to behold. He should possess great wealth and large property with stores of silver, gold, aids to enjoyment, corn and with his treasure-houses and garners. He should be powerful, in command of loyal and disciplined army. The king should be a believer, a generous person, and a noble giver. He should learn all branches of knowledge, know the meaning of what would have been said and could explain the meaning of the doctrine. He should be intelligent, expert and wise, and able to think out objects present or past or future. A king's noble thoroughbred steed was said to be worthy of the king having possessed of beauty, strength and speed. Further, according to the *Nikāyas*, a king should possess five qualities which were reckoned to be his assets. These were: straightness (*ajjava*), swiftness (*javana*), gentleness (*maddava*), patience (*khanti*), and restraint (*soracca*). He should have good knowledge of wealth, virtue, measure, time and the assembled men (Barua, 1971, pp. 194-95).

Duties of a Good King / Ideal King

As regards the noble duty of a king it is said that he should lean on the norm (the law of truth and righteousness), honour, respect and revere it, do homage to it, hallow it; being himself a norm-banner, a norm-signal, having the norm (*Dhamma*) as his master, he should provide the right watch, ward and protection for his own folk, for the army, for the nobles, for vassals, for Brahmanas, and householders, for town and country dwellers, for the religious world, and for beasts and birds. The sacred duty of the king was to be pleasing to the Brahmanas and the householders who in turn should respect him as the father. The king should base his daily life upon the single principle (*ekodhammo*) of watchfulness (*appamado*), for he would thereby keep himself active and wakeful and guard his family members, vassal kings, treasury and store-house. There should not be prevailed wrong-doing throughout his kingdom. And whoever in his kingdom would be poor, to him the wealth should be given (Barua, 1971, p. 198).

As a righteous king it was his solemn duty to protect all citizens from injustice and to be impartial in his application of legal concepts. The king had to save not only his kingdom against invaders, but also life, property and traditional custom against internal disruptive forces. He had also to protect the family organisation from its utter destruction by punishing adultery, ensuring the fair inheritance of family wealth, supporting the widows, and orphans, suppressing robbery and protecting the poor from the greedy hands of the rich. The *Dīgha Nikāya* relates that the king should supply food, seeds, capital, and wages to the followers of the various occupations according to their needs; he should accordingly protect them from want and disorder as well as increased revenues and should establish peace (Barua, 1971, p. 198).

He had also to be frequently engaged in wars and to quell frontier-rebellions and to act as the commander-in-chief of the state army. During peace-time, his duty was, however, to deliver the administration of justice. He used to become often an original tribunal and conduct the cases in his court not only as the highest and ultimate judicial authority, but also as a direct court of appeal and the nearest legal authority without any intermediate institution. No exact demarcation may be made as to the cases referred to the king and the judges. A *Kshatriya*, or a *Brahmana*, or a *Vessa* or a *Sudda* who was considered to be guilty of theft or house-breaking or adultery should usually be brought up for sentence before a king who might put him to death or confiscate his property or banish him or otherwise deal with him without any consideration for caste, creed or sex. Because as soon as a person would commit an offence, he would lose his former designation like *Kshatriya* or *Brahmana* and would be treated simply as a man (Barua, 1971, pp. 198 - 199).

About the Buddhist ideal of kingship Saletore writes that: the Buddhists denied that one of the duties of the king was to maintain the social order and to see that the four *Varnas* and the four *Asramas* were confined to their respective spheres of duties. Similarly, the Buddhists denied the restriction of kingship to the *Kshatriyas* in the Social Order, for them the *Kshatriyas* were to be called so primarily because they looked after the fields. They disbelieved in the sanctity that surrounded the person of the king, whom they would describe only as one who was elected by common consent – *Mahasammata*. This would seem to rule out the possibility of hereditary among the kings of the Buddhist mould. To the Buddhists, sword was merely an ornament so that other things might wait on the monarch respectfully for orders. In politics, therefore, Buddhism definitely discouraged the pretension of kings to divine or semi-divine status. When the *Brahmanical* literature often declared that the kings were partial incarnations of the gods and encouraged an attitude of passive obedience to them, the *Pali Nikāyas* categorically proclaimed that the first king was merely the chosen leader of the people, appointed by them to restrain crime and protect property, and that his right to levy taxation depended not on birth or succession but on the efficient performance of his duties. In this sense Buddhism had a rational attitude for mitigating the autocracy of the Indian king, even though it did not formulate any distinctive system of political ethics (Saletore, 1963, p. 326).

A good king is expected to be charitable, moral, sacrificing, just, humble, penitent, non-wrathful, nonviolent, patient and harmless. However, a good king should also subserve the traditions of *attha* and *dhamma*. The terms *attha* and *dhamma* may be rendered as actions conducive to prosperity and righteousness. The *Jatakas* mention there was a specific officer whose task was to advise the king on *attha* and *dhamma (attha dhamma nusasakamcco)*. *Dhamma* is often equated with *sama* which may be translated as impartiality and a sense of justice. In fact, the ideal king is often called *dhammikodhamaraja*.The king is expected to protect the people against foreign aggression and any form of internal disorder or oppression and to administer impartial justice. The Ministers should help the king in the performance of his duty.

In the *Rathalatthi Jataka* it has been mentioned that the Minister of justice who happened to be the Bodhisattva, the

Buddha in a past life, impresses on the king the necessity of due investigation into a case before pronouncing the sentence. "A lazy fellow given to sensual indulgence is not good, an ascetic who does not control himself is no good, a king is not good who acts without investigation, a wise man who is angry is also not good. The king should act after he has heard, O ruler Honour and fame fall to the lot of him who acts after investigation, O king" (Prasad, 1974, p. 209).

Features of Buddhist Polity

1. Concept of Sovereignty

When a king is endowed with the above mentioned qualities, he rightfully enjoys sovereignty. The concept of sovereignty is expressed through the use of five distinct terms – *vasa, adhipacca, anubhava, siri* and *issariya*. Of these *vasa* means power, authority, control and influence; *adhipacca* may be translated as supreme rule, power, lordship and sovereignty (it signifies overlordship, the quality of imposing superiority over others); *anubhava* stands for influence, control and power; *siri* is splendour, beauty, good fortune, glory, majesty and prosperity and is based on material possessions (*siri bhoganam asayo*); *issariya* is the quality of exercising overwhelming influence or control, the capacity to impose sovereignty (rulership, supremacy and dominion). All of them collectively imply a condition of sovereign power capable of giving orders to all and receiving orders from none. It is a condition of pre-eminence in power relationships which carries along with it certain well-defined obligations which are the duties of the office of kingship. But it is not mere physical or material power for there is invariably associated with kingship a spiritual power or a "charisma". This spiritual power is variously acquired and manifests itself through diverse symbols.

2. Constituent Organs of Sovereignty

The sovereignty of the state is manifested through its many constituent organs. The Buddhists do not offer a systematised list of constituents of the state. However, there are several passages which contain suggestions which, taken together, may give us the Buddhist ideas on the constituents of the state. Of these the king, naturally, is the leading constituent. Next to him comes territory (*rattha*). This is followed by the mention of the bureaucracy (*amacca* and *parisajja*), the armed forces (*balam*) the treasury (*kosakotthagara*), allies (*anuyuttakhattiya* and *kuddarajano*) and the people (*manussa*). Some of these have their own subdivisions. For instance, the territorial organisation is often described as fourfold, comprising villages (*gama*), market towns (*nigama*), countryside (*janapada*) and city (*nagara*). The people are supposed to have four different Assemblies (*parisas*), one each for the *Kshatriyas*, *Brahmanas*, householders (*gahapati*) and ascetics (*samana*). Sometimes another element is added to the list of the components of the territory and it is the frontier (*paccanta*) whose security is always a matter of anxiety for it is often in a state of rebellion (*kupita*) (Gokhale, 1994, p. 125).

3. Symbols of Sovereignty

It is unique to Buddhism. The important symbols of sovereignty are:

Cakka (Wheel of Power)

The wheel is likened to the disc of the sun and is more a mystical symbol than a material object. In order that it may appear before him, a *Cakkavatti* has to keep the *uposatha*(fast and penance) on the full moon day, purify himself and mediate. It his personal acquisition and cannot be handed down in succession and it sinks or slips down a little as the king approaches the end of his life.

Hathi (Elephant)

The elephant (*uposatho nagaraja*) is described as all white, sevenfold strong, with strength equal to that of 10,000 men, firm, wonderful in power and capable of flying through the air.

Assa (Horse)

The horse is also all white with a crow-black head and a dark mane and able to fly

Parinayakal (Prime Minister)

Itthi (Woman or Wife)

Mani (Precious Gems or Jewels)

The jewel is bright and beautiful, eight-faced, well-cut, four cubits in thickness and in circumference like the nave of a cart-wheel. Its brilliance is such that it surpasses all and spreads around for a league on every side.

Gahapatia (Steward)

4. The White Umbrella

The umbrella is pure white and stainless, with a handle of firm wood and with many hundreds of ribs. All these seem to represent the material accessories of a powerful monarch. It is evident that the whole symbolism is in some ways associated with powers of nature, especially the sun. This paraphernalia is secured not through the performance of any Vedic sacrifices but through piety, morality and mystic contemplation. It is not necessarily a gift from some divine source but may be obtained by anyone who is morally elevated, spiritually pure and intellectually and mentally dedicated to morality or *dhamma*.

Buddhist Society is Just Society which Opposes *Brahmanic* Society

In the *Assalayana Sutta*, the Buddha ridicules the *Brahmanic* claim that they were born of the mouth of the Brahma (*purusa*), pointing out that the wives of the *Brahmanas* too were seen to be pregnant and giving birth to children in the same way as the wives of men of other classes. Again the story of *AsitaDevala* narrated in the same *Sutta* convincingly proves that the *Brahmanic* claim to superiority on grounds of birth was meaningless. In the same

Sutta, the Buddha points out that contrary to the traditional four-fold division of society which the *Brahmins* claimed to be absolute, there were in some societies such as *Yona* and *Kamboja*, only two classes (Dissanayake, 2009, p. 13).

In order to assert the conception of the equality of man the Buddha pointed out that even a Śudra, who could command wealth easily employ as his servant a *Brahmana* or a *Kshatriya* or a *Vaisya* to attend to him and to his menial household work. Therefore, there was no intrinsic reason why anyone particular group of persons should be born to serve others. To counter the *Brahmanic* argument that only people belonging to certain specific castes were capable of performing certain specific functions, the Buddha quite sarcastically stated that people of all castes, whether high or low were capable of kindling a fire and added that a fire kindled by a so-called 'low' caste person was not less bright than a fire kindled by a so-called 'high' caste. The reference to the fire was apparently a sarcastic reference to the *Brahmanas* because kindling sacrificial fires was claimed to be the specific function of the *Brahmanas* assigned to them by God. (Dissanayake, 2009, pp. 13-14).

Buddhism represents a revolt against *Brahmanism*. Buddhist social theory confers no privileges on *Brahmanas*. It denies sanctity to those who commonly passed as *Brahmanas*. Referring obviously to *Brahmanic* practices, the northern *Dhammapada*, an anthology of verses taken chiefly from five *Nikāyas*, remarks that nakedness, long hair, dirt, fasting, sleeping on the ground or sitting motionless does not bring purity and does not resolve doubts. One does not become a *Brahmana* by his family, by his long locks, by his lineage. Real *Brahmanas* are those who are endowed with virtue and purity and who know the law. The *MajjhimaNikāya* admits the primacy of the *Brahmanas* and *Kshatriyas* in social etiquette, but later in the dialogue of the *MadhuraSutta*, it expressly denies the utility of caste in securing happiness in this life or in the next. It denies caste privilege before the law and more than anything else insists that caste is wholly immaterial in ascetic life. In the *Dīgha Nikāya*, a *Brahmana*, Ambattha, repeats the current *Brahmanical* doctrine that *Kshatriyas, Vaisyas* and Śudras had been created to serve *Brahmanas* but the Buddha does not admit the claim and silences the interrogator by some awkward questions on his own parentage. In the same dialogue, *Kshatriyas* are shown to be higher than *Brahmanas* (Prasad, 1974, pp. 209-210).

Thus the most important features of Buddhist society is the absolute equality of all its members. For Buddhism, all men being equal, birth does not originate any difference among them in terms of hierarchy or grant them any particular privilege. It is not surprising that the Buddha admitted in his community (*Sangha*) persons coming from all the levels of the Indian society. The provenance of some of the most important and respected members of the Buddhist Order were castes considered by *Brahmanism* as low and impure. For instance, Upali, one of the most eminent disciples of the Buddha, was the son of a barber. Upali was the monk most versed in the norms of monastic discipline (*Vinaya*). Among the disciples of the Buddha were also Angulimala, a robber who was converted by the Buddha, and Ambapali, a courtesan of Vesali, who alternated, in equal conditions, with the Brahmans that in great number entered the Buddhist Order, abandoning prejudices and privileges, and putting at the service of Buddhism their intellectual and literary training. (Dragonetti, 2013, pp. 36, 39).

For people of low castes to enter Buddhist community was the recovery of their human dignity which had been denied to them in *Brahmanic* society. Once inside the Buddhist community they were treated as human beings, as equal to the other human beings, with the same capacity, rights and opportunities all human beings have for the achievements of their noblest aspirations in this life and in future lives. As important consequence of the disappearance of the castes, Buddhism teaches "an ethic valid for everybody" (*Dharma*), opposed to the *Brahmanic* ethic constituted by the "One's own duty" (*Svadharma*). Thus

Buddhist society is a society with features essentially opposed to those of the *Brahmanic* society, and, what is most important, a more just society, because it proclaims the equality of all human beings and denies that birth and belonging to a social group grant rights and privileges. From this point of view Buddhism meant a "revolution" in the Indian society before the beginning of the Common Era, revolution deprived of any violence, which tried to transform society in ancient India. Buddha's conception of society and his rejection of the castes system is in absolute congruency with his attitude of universalistic inclusivism (not to leave anyone outside) and generosity (not to keep for oneself the riches of any nature). With the lapse of centuries Buddha's teachings about the conception of society have not lost their wisdom and capacity to benefit people. Today in a great number of countries it is still birth that determines the destiny of persons. There a boy, or a girl, born in a poor family has scanty possibilities to avoid a life of poverty and suffering. Birth makes them forever. (Dragonetti, 2013, p. 41).

Judicial Administration

A discourse in the *Majjhima Nikāya* enumerates in details the punishments for offences. It is said that there were some persons who might break into a house and carry off the booty, behave as a thief, wait in ambush and go to other man's wife. As regards the punishment for such offences it was said that the king having arrested the guilty dealt out various punishments: he would lash him with whips, canes, birch rods; he would cut off his hand, foot, hand and foot both, ear, nose, ear and nose both; he would offer him the 'gruel pot' 'the shell-tonsure', 'Rahu's mouth, the 'fire garland', the flaming hand', the 'hay twist', the 'bark dress', the 'antelope', 'flesh-hooking, the 'disc-slice', the 'pickling process', 'circling the pin', 'straw mattress punishments'; he would spray him with boiling oil, give him as food to the dogs, impale him alive on stakes and decapitate him with a sword. Thus the guilty persons had to undergo various punishments for their offences at the hands of the kings (Barua, 1971, pp. 240-241).

In the Lichchavi *Gana* we find that there was a judicial Minister who could be even an outsider, a paid officer. The right of freedom of the citizens was cautiously protected.

A citizen would be guilty only when he was considered so by the President, Vice-President, and Commander-in-Chief separately and without any difference of opinion. The record of the decisions of the President was carefully kept on the rolls in which particulars of crime and punishment awarded to the guilty persons was recorded. In the Court of Justice who formed the regular court for civil cases and ordinary offences was held the preliminary enquiry. But the Court of Appeal was usually presided over by the Lawyer Judges. The Judges of the High Court were known as the Doctors of Law. There was a Council of Final Appeal named the *Atthakulaka* (Court of the Eight). One of these courts could announce that a citizen was innocent. Even if all the courts would declare any citizen guilty, the matter could still be subject to the decision of the members of the Executive Cabinet. Thus the *Atthakulaka* evidently denoted a judicial council of eight members, and not, the "Representative of eight clans" (Barua, 1971, pp. 211-212).

Military Administration

In the *Nikāyas* we find that due to frequent wars and frontier troubles, each state had to maintain a well-trained military force like modern states for defence purposes. There was the traditional division of an army into four component parts viz. chariots, elephants, cavalry and infantry. The chariot was probably the most important apparatus of war. Elephants also played an important role in the war-fields of ancient India and served the purpose of tanks, breaking up the enemy's ranks and destroying palisades, gates, etc. It is often found that when the king used to lead an army against his enemy, usually he took his seat on the state-elephant. An ideal war-elephant was strongly-tusked and best when sixty years old being 'a type of male vigour'. Sometimes a line of elephants might also act as a living bridge for crossing rivulets and streams.

Fighting elephants might at first create great terror in an invading army being by no means invincible. We find that even the highly trained elephants could easily be demoralised, particularly by fire. During peace, the elephants were colourfully decorated for grand processions (Barua, 1971, pp. 214-216).

In the ancient period Horsemen as also in the Middle Ages formed one of the vital parts of the national army. The war-horses were clad in iron-armour and mail, while the cavalry-men were usually armed with swords and bows. The foot-soldiers were probably recruited from the *Kshatriyas* who were loyal to the state. They were clad in mail-coats in order to save themselves from the attacks of the sharp arrows and similar other dangerous missiles. However, the soldiers were well-equipped with numerous weapons like the bows, swords, spears, etc. and put on the robes of different colours in order to befool the enemies. Most of them were highly trained in archery. It is said that the foot-soldiers were usually expert in fighting. The entire army organisation was divided into several divisions which were possibly under different generals, but the whole army was in general supervision and control of the Commander-in-Chief who usually belonged to the ruling family occupying an important place among the Ministers of the state and in the war-fields holding the next highest military post after the king. But during the peace-time he acted generally as a judge looking after due protection of life and property of the citizens (Barua, 1971, pp. 216-217).

The art of warfare together with its various tactics, stratagems and practices are also found mentioned in the *Nikāyas*. When the armies stationed on the borders failed to cope with the situation, they used to send letters describing in details to the king who immediately would proceed to the scene of operations. As a fight would become imminent, the armies were usually advised to assemble for the purpose by beats of martial drums. The pay of the soldiers was generally a portion of the booty in war. The army during its march used to set up camps. The warfare was generally concentrated around the capital, other parts of the country being little affected by it. Generally at a specific season the army would start on a campaign marching in regular bands. The soldiers used to occupy a suitable place not far from the city intended for attack. Prior to the actual beginning of war the *purohita* and other wise sages who would accompany the army or the leader or the king himself used to deliver a short but passionate speech in order to encourage the soldiers to fight (Barua, 1971, p. 218).

The siege-warfare was the general practice. The aggressive king would besiege his neighbour's capital and take the offensive with the call of "either surrender or battle". If the latter did not surrender, the former would advance besieging him. Next the invading king used to direct his army against the ditches and order the soldiers to disperse all about the city, fill up the trenches, break down the walls, raze the gate-towers, enter the city, and deal with the people's heads like pumpkins cast on a cart. Sometimes during the warfare by means of blockade the supplies of bare necessities of life to the besieged city were stopped by the invading army. Due to blockade many nations usually had to surrender their freedom and sovereignty at the feet of the enemies. Further, a noteworthy characteristic of the siege-warfare was a regular system of espionage. That's why spies were regularly employed to which the activities in the enemy's camp and to supply secret reports. They carefully mixed up with the enemies to know the secrets, and sowed the seed of dissension by lies among the enemy soldiers. With regards to the war-ethics, we find that like the present warfare a messenger or ambassador was not generally attacked. Possibly the wounded soldiers in war were carried away on stretchers and properly treated (Barua, 1971, pp. 219-220).

Rural Administration

It was observed that the bulk of the people even then dwelt in the villages. The villagers used to concentrate in a relatively small area as their dwellings were all clustered together to ensure safety. The rural administration was based on "peasant proprietorship".

But no owner could sell or mortgage his part of the land without the consent of the village council. The villagers were generally endowed with a sturdy civic spirit. They united themselves in such undertakings as laying irrigational channels, building mote-halls, rest-houses, etc. On the whole, it may be said that each village was a self-sufficient unit in the midst of simple unsophisticated surroundings (Barua, 1971, pp. 220-221).

As regards the internal administration we find that the village enjoyed a fair amount of autonomy due to the non-interfering policy of the central government. Each village was generally under the supervision of its headsman known as the governor of village who held a very important position in the village administration. The village headman occupied normally a hereditary position, though he was frequently looked on as the king's representative. He was usually one of the wealthier peasants, and was remunerated with tax-free land or dues in kind or both. In the larger villages he was a very important functionary, with a small staff of village officials, such as an accountant, a watchman and tax collector. The village headman appeared as the champion of the villagers and was responsible for the defence of the village. He used to exercise even judicial and executive powers in certain civil as well as criminal cases. Sometimes he seemed to be an oppressive local tyrant. In such cases the villagers could apply to the king for protection against the wicked headman. So the power of the village headman was not unlimited. Every possibility of his being a tyrant in his own village was controlled. He was even ultimately responsible to the king for his decisions and had little power to inflict graver punishment. In judicial affairs the final authority mainly vested in the king or his court. As one of the litigant parties in a village would desire redress at the hands of the king or his court, in spite of suitable arrangements in the village itself he could do so, and the case had to be decided accordingly. If the other party would deny to agree with such a procedure, he would be liable to punishment. Thus the rural administration was evidently linked up with the central government (Barua, 1971, p. 222).

Every village had an Assembly of its own exercising a great influence on the activities of the headman. However, the number of members of the Village Assembly was varied. The Assembly was a potent force in the settlement of affairs affecting the common interests of the villagers in general. The meetings of the Village Assembly were generally held in a hall in the midst of the village provided with boards, seats and a jar of water. Thus, the village administration was largely carried on by the Assembly with the help of the headman. The central government did not interfere much in the rural affairs save the graver judicial matters and the revenue collection. So the village enjoyed the privileges of self-government (Barua, 1971, pp. 222-223).

Dhamma as a Political Concept

A random search for the varieties of *Dhamma*'s meanings and usage reveals that it has more than seventeen different connotations. *Dhamma* may mean a precondition or a distinguishing attribute, a factor of personality or a state of mind, an ethical quality or an entire system of salvation, a theory in general or earthly existence, a hypothetical construct or a practical precept, Buddhist *Nibbana*, equity, merit, non-violence, compassion, a code of conduct for social groups or individuals including kings (Gokhale, 1994, p. 146). The purpose here is to examine the content of *Dhamma* in its political connotations or to deal with the role of the concept of *Dhamma* in the early Buddhist ideas on the nature and functions of the state.

For the early Buddhists the two essential and inseparable parts of the institutions of the state were the material and moral welfare of its subjects. The central problem in all their speculations on the nature and functions of the state was the violence, force, and arbitrariness inherent in the exercise of its power. The reality of the power of the state was often likely to manifest itself in the violence of wars or expropriation and arbitrary conduct influenced by despotic ambitions of individual rulers. The early Buddhists saw a solution to it by making *Dhamma* its basis in the hope that a constant awareness of *Dhamma* would transform the very nature of the state. So, in the political sense *Dhamma* meant the ten ethical qualities of a king comprising character, charity, renunciation, uprightness, gentleness, non-anger, austerity, non-injury, forbearance, non-opposition. The king must know and cultivate the qualities of discretion with regard to welfare, law, moderation, time, and counsel. Further, he should avoid untruth, levity, be of an amiable disposition, mindful, courageous, and a protector of all. Such a psychological preparation alone would enable the king to comprehend what is *Dhamma* and how to associate it with the everyday tasks of government. It is this combination of *Dhamma* as a theory of royal conduct with procedure or method that makes a king a moral being which was the ultimate object of the early Buddhist political theory (Gokhale, 1994, p. 151).

The Buddhists envisage the state essentially in its relationships with the family led by the *gahapati*, the group of *religiux* comprising the *Brahmanas*, *samanas*, *paribbajakas* and the *Sakyaputtiyasamanas* led by their respective leaders and councils (parisa) and the diverse civic associations such as the *mantriparisa*, the *negamas* and *janapadas*. Each group must base its conduct on the dictates of *Dhamma*. For the gahapati the Buddha laid down a *gahapativinaya* and exhorted him to acquire wealth by exertion and energy, by the strength of his own arms and earned in the sweat of his own brow. Therefore, *Dhamma* was to be the common and ultimate basis of all social relationships presided over by the state (Gokhale, 1994, p. 152).

Dhamma is considered as an all-pervasive, inexorable, indestructible and eternal mystic entity. In this aspect *Dhamma* stood above and beyond the state. In an illuminating passage, when asked by a *bhikkhu* as to who was the ruler of rulers, the Buddha is reported to have replied that it was Dhamma. The ideal ruler is declared to rule depending on *Dhamma*, respecting it, worshipping it, with *Dhamma* as his banner and pennant, with *Dhamma* as his lord. Every one of his actions in his relations with every category of beings, even unto the birds and beasts, must be informed by the letter and spirit of this *Dhamma* for otherwise his rule becomes anarchy. It is *Dhamma* that curbs the intoxication of power, from which the king is very likely to suffer, and avert misfortune to himself and his subjects (Gokhale, 1994, p. 152).

As *rajadhamma* it is simply a code of proper ethical behaviour for a king. It defines his prerogatives and the conditions under which he may use them. Since each constituent element of the state, the family, the various *parisas* and sundry groups, has its own *dhamma*, the whole of society is closely integrated in is web. In this context, *Dhamma* is ideal behaviour, strongly recommended for acceptance and practice on every side (Gokhale, 1994, p. 152).

Dhamma is a cosmic force, inexorable, eternal and inescapable. It exists in its own right beyond and above the state. It sanctions are supra-natural and assume a cosmic retributive character. A king who violates the dictates of this *Dhamma* invites wrath of nature and the gods upon himself, his subjects and his realm. In retaliation against such a king the heavenly bodies such as the sun, moon, and the constellations, suspend their natural functions. The natural order of the seasons of day and night is profoundly disturbed. The fruits and fruit grains, honey and sugar, oils and condiments lose their natural flavour and nourishing qualities. The ministers, judicial officers and men of law and order become despotic and corrupt and anarchy reigns supreme. The people in their disgust either immigrate in large numbers to another state or rise in rebellion. Finally the deities themselves become wrathful and destroy the errant king (Gokhale, 1994, p. 153).

Dhamma gives us the early Buddhist idea of the basis of allegiance in relationships between the state and its citizens. The *Mahasammata* story indicates that the basis of allegiance is the agreement between the ruler and the subjects by which the ruler undertakes to impose a law and order and the subjects, in their turn, agree to pay him taxes and obey his orders. This has been interpreted as a kind of a primitive contract. With the development of the theory of *Dhamma* this theory of contract is superceded. *Dhamma* exists prior to the contract even before the hypothetical "golden age", a fall from which led to the emergence of the state. It operates eternally and beyond the wishes of the king or his subjects. It is supreme ruler, the ruler of rulers. It cannot be a subject of contractual relationship. It gives the king the authority to rule and calls upon the subjects to obey him so long as the king abides by its wishes. It watches over the king at all times and hence is a quasi-cosmic force working in its own mysterious way. It forms the ultimate nexus between the state and the citizens. The citizens must obey the ruler as long and only as long as he obeys *Dhamma*. When he ceases to do that the basis of allegiance is destroyed and rebellion becomes inevitable. *Dhamma* stands between order and anarchy; it transforms the condition of non-state into state. It protects the institutions of property and family and is the source of all the rules of conduct pertaining to the diverse groups within the society (Gokhale, 1994, p. 153).

Concept of Political Economy Governance: *Cakkavattin* or Universal Ruler

Cakkavatti Sihanada Sutta of the *Dīgha Nikāya* says that the society was perfectly happy and peaceful as long as the king (government) provided all living beings with the necessary protection (by maintaining law and order) and ensured the people's material and moral well-being. So the *Sutta* has tried its best by narrating the story of a universal monarch by throwing much light upon the correlation between politics and economics on the one hand and social-moral significance of the political economy on the other hand.

In the past there was a universal monarch who ruled the world righteously. In the central hall of his palace there was a Celestial Wheel (*Cakka*) which symbolised his authority. This wheel moved from its usual position or vanished altogether when the king failed in his royal duty or when the time came for the Monarch to retire. One day the king, on being informed that the Celestial Wheel had slipped down from its usual position, realised that the time had come for him to hand over the reins of government to his heir. He summoned his eldest son and having established him on the throne, donned the robes of a hermit and left home for a homeless state. But on the seventh day of the new king's coronation, the Celestial Wheel disappeared. The king got excited and rushed to his father in the forest and informed him of the disappearance of the Celestial Wheel. The ex-king then explained that no monarch inherited the Celestial Wheel from his parents and that each one had to qualify himself to earn the Wheel, adding that if he conformed to the noble ideal of a *Cakkavatti* king, the Celestial Wheel would reappear in the palace. On being asked what the noble ideal of a *Cakkavatti* king was, the ex-king said that a *Cakkavatti* king must always be guided by the *Dhamma*. Acting in accordance with the *Dhamma*, he must provide all living beings in the kingdom with protection from law-breakers and deter the people from evil ways. He must also ensure their economic welfare (Dissanayake, 2009, p. 19).

Then the king returned to his kingdom and acted accordingly and the Celestial Wheel reappeared in the palace. When he paid it the due respects, the Wheel began to roll onwards to the East and the king followed it together with his army. Whenever the Wheel stopped, all the rival kings in the East came up to him and welcomed him with open arms and acknowledged him as their emperor. Similarly, the Celestial Wheel in turn rolled on to the South, West and the North followed by the king and his army. The rival kings in those regions too welcomed him and acknowledged him as their emperor. The vassal kings then asked for instructions from the Emperor who thereupon issued the following five commandments: "You shall not kill living beings; You shall not take that which has not been given; You shall not act wrongly touching bodily desires; You shall speak no lie; You shall not drink maddening drink; enjoy your possessions as you have been won't to do." In like manner, seven *Cakkavatti* kings of that lineage ruled the world for several thousand years. Under their rule, social and economic injustices were unheard of and the people of the whole world lived in peace and amity as members of a single family. Above all, the entire world was unified under one system of administration based on conquest by righteousness (*dhamma-vijaya*) which totally rejected the scourge of war and violence (Dissanayake, 2009, pp. 19 - 20).

The *Kutadanta Sutta* of the *Dīgha Nikāya* describes the causes of crime and futility of meting out punishment to eradicate it. Instead, the Buddha suggests that in order to eradicate crime, the economic conditions of the people should be improved, farmers should be given the necessary facilities for agriculture, traders should be provided with capital, employees should be paid adequate wages and salaries and those who are in financial distress should be exempted from tax. When people are provided with opportunities to earn an adequate income, the need to resort to stealing, lying and violence and other social evils will disappear, and consequently, the country will be peaceful (Dissanayake, 2009, p. 21).

The Aggañña Sutta categorically states that the human society reached its lowest ebb after the establishment of the institution of private property and the consequent rise of individualism (*Atta*). Therefore, Buddha seemed to have favoured a society in which all property of significant value was socially owned and distributed strictly in accordance with the individual needs of its members. Both the *CakkavattiSihanada* and *KutadantaSuttas* make it amply clear that the Buddha recognised economic welfare as being of paramount importance for social stability, peace and good government. At the same time, the three *Suttas* equally emphatically demonstrate that moral turpitude makes social stability, peace and good government impossible. Therefore, we could conclude that both poverty as well as craving for wealth in excess of what is absolutely necessary for living could corrupt society, and should be avoided. It follows then that economic well-being and morality are essential attributes of a healthy social order (Dissanayake, 2009, pp. 21-22). The rearing of cattle and agriculture formed the principal economic activity. Land was owned in common by the villagers or by the tribal chief who worked them by hired labour. Frequent references in the canonical texts to trade and crafts such as pottery, carpentry, textile weaving as well as centres of trade suggests the existence of a cottage industrial system and a network of city centres (Dissanayake, 2009, p. 24).

Republican Features

Monarchy was the prevailing form of government during the Vedic period. In the post-Vedic days a change in the form of government became visible and monarchy in some parts of India made room for certain non-monarchical states which were generally known as republics. So in ancient Indian terms for 'Republic' were probably *'Gana'* and *'Sangha'* which certainly implied the "rule by many", "rule of numbers", "government by assembly or parliament". In the *Majjhima Nikāya* the terms *Gana* and *Sangha* are used side by side to mean the Republics. Republics of ancient India were of mainly two types, namely, those which were constituted by the whole or a section of a single clan (*kula*), e.g. the *Sakiyas*, the *Koliyas*, the *Mallas* of Kusinara and Pava and those which consisted of several clans, namely, the Vajjis, the *Yadavas*, etc. But the chief characteristic of an Indian republic was the absence of one single hereditary monarch who exercised sovereign control over it. He was elected as office-holder presiding over the sessions in public assembly and over the state. But it is not certain how and for what period he was chosen. He was generally called a *Raja*. Thus we find that at one time Bhaddiya, a young cousin of Buddha was known as the *Raja*, while Suddhodana, Buddha's father who was designated as the *Raja* to whom was assisted by a council of archons chosen from the ruling class. Some of the republics maintained an elaborate system of judicial procedure with a gradation of officers. Again some others including the *Koliyas* possessed a police force which was ill-famed for extortion and violence (Barua, 1971, pp. 201, 204, 206).

The most noteworthy institution of these republics was the popular assembly, at which the young and the old were present for discussion on settlements of communal affairs. The Lichchavis were governed by an assembly of their own, but they had leaders who were not members of it. This indicates that there were separate chiefs. Thus it may be noted that while there might have been corporations among the Lachchavis, they had different clans which had leaders of their own. There were many small towns and villages in the *Sakiya* state, which had their own Assemblies meeting in their Assembly Halls (*Santhagara*). According to A.S. Altekar, in these "assemblies the non-privileged classes may have had an equal voice in local affairs". It may further be observed that the Assembly Halls occasionally represented the social clubs where social and religious questions were considered. According to B.A. Saletore, the Central Assembly consisted of two houses, one Upper and the other Lower, which controlled even the foreign policy, entertained ambassadors and foreign princes, discussed their proposal and settled the issues of peace and war. The members used to follow a definite procedure relating to the business of the Assembly which was represented by the parties and required a quorum for deciding issues. There was also an Executive Council under the constitutional control of the Central Assembly. The appointments to the state services and the governorship of the provinces might have been approved by the Central Assembly. Buddha, who had a sympathetic look on the republics warned the people against the dissension and gave constructive suggestions for peace, harmony, and unity (Barua, 1971, pp. 207 -209).

In an ideal *Gana* state meetings were characterised by concord and harmony and the opinions of the elders occasionally decided the minor issues. Such a practice was also in vogue among the Lichchavis during the golden period of their republican constitution. Thus in course of time some rules of procedure had been evolved as regards the debates and working of the Assembly. As the differences of opinion would occur in the Assemblies, votes were taken and the majority view was generally honoured. It is found that when the *Sakiyas* received the ultimatum from the Kosalan king, who was besieging their capital, they assembled in the Assembly to discuss whether they should open the gates or not. There some agreed with the proposal, others disagreed. As a result votes were taken to ascertain the majority will (Barua, 1971, p. 209).

In the popular assembly members were generally seated in specified order. After the president had laid the proposed business before the assembly, others spoke upon it and then was recorded the unanimous decision arrived at. If there appeared any disputation or controversy, the matter was usually referred to a committee of arbitrators. It is presumed that the technical terms like seat-betokener, motion, ballot-collector, whip, and referendum appeared in the Rules of the Buddhist monks were probably adopted from those in use in the Assemblies of the clans (Barua, 1971, p. 210).

There were three highest officers, namely, the President, the vice-president and the commander-in-chief. The *Jataka* adds a fourth called the Chancellor of the Exchequer. It may be that these four highest administrative officers constituted the cabinet or executive authority. The rule, as in the case of the Lichchavis vested in the inhabitants, 7707 in number all of whom were entitled to rule and often used to hold the highest offices of the state. Thus it is evident that 7707 of the inhabitants possibly the foundation families formed the ruling class (Barua, 1971, p. 210).

When the Vesalians used to come to their House of Law (Parliament), the tocsin was usually sounded. Generally, political, military, agricultural and even commercial matters were discussed in the House of Law. Description is also found of the Lichchavi *Gana* in session appointing a distinguished member to be the envoy, charging him to deliver a message "on behalf of the Lichchavis of Vesali", i.e. the *Gana* transacted business on behalf of the whole people. In the Council of the Vesalians every member had an equal right of speech and voting; and everyone wanted to be the next President who was also the highest judicial authority (Barua, 1971, p. 211).

In the *Maha Parinibbana Sutta* we find occasional references to qualifications of the citizens of a republican community. It is said that when Ajatasattu, the king of Magadha, had made up his mind by attacking to annex the Vajjian Republic to his kingdom and sent his Minister to the Buddha for his advice he was told by Buddha that the Vajjians could not be subjugated as long as they observe seven conditions of welfare viz. so long as the Vajjis would foregather often and frequent the public meetings of their clan; so long as the Vajjis would meet together, rise, and carry out their undertakings in concord; so long as they would enact nothing already established, abrogate nothing that had been enacted, and act in accordance with the ancient institutions; so long as they would honour, esteem, revere and support the elders and hold it a point of duty to listen to their words; so long as no women or girls belonging to other clans would be detained among them by force or abduction; so long as they would honour, esteem, revere and support the shrines in towns and country by allowing proper offerings and rites; and lastly so long as they would rightfully protect and support *Arahats* among them (Barua, 1971, p. 213). These seven conditions were the pillars of strength and prosperity of the Vajjan Republic. These conditions indirectly emphasised certain qualifications of good citizenship in a republican state. Thus the strict observance of these conditions guaranteed for them an ideal society. Therefore we may conclude that public spiritedness (indicated by frequent attendance and unity at the assembly), wisdom (shown by loyalty to customs and traditions), morality (indicated by seemly behaviour towards women), discipline (reflected by respect shown to elders), piety (shown by respect for the shrines), and protection of the saints, constituted the principles adopted by a republican *Sangha* in the sixth century B.C. in India (Dissanayake, 2009, p. 26).

Professor Ling says "the weakness of the republics is demonstrated by the fact that their collapse followed within a few years of the Buddha's death, that is by about the middle of the fifth century B.C. While this was due partly to the aggression of the monarchies, it was due in fairly large measure to internal disagreements among the republican nobles or elders, and to the moral indolence, lack of discipline and justice, and an ill-founded pride. Therefore, in general the collapse of the republics may be said to have been due to the prevalence of an undisciplined individualism" (Dissanayake, 2009, p. 26).

Conclusion

The preceding analysis underlines that 'Buddha' is not a name but a 'Title' which means 'a person who is awake'. Gautama Buddha himself never claimed to be God. The Buddha was a 'human being' who became tolerant and enlightened. He taught the way to Enlightenment to many others.

Buddhist account of the origin of the state or kingship is closely linked with its account of the evolution of the universe. According to *Dīgha Nikāya*, an important Buddhist scripture, with the appearance of high-quality rice and its consumption, men acquire physical strength. These results in the rise of passions among men and women who tend to build households and store rice. This tendency gives rise to scarcity situation whereupon men decide to divide and demarcate their rice fields. Now certain greedy being, while guarding his own rice-plot, steals another's plot and makes use of it. Thereupon others arrest and censure him for this act. They make him promise not to do it again. But he resorts to lying and repeats the act when he is struck by others. Thus four evils come into existence: theft, censure, lying and violence. Thereupon, the people gather together to deliberate on the ways to control these evils. They decide to select a person who should be wrathful when indignation is justified; who should censure the person that must be censured; and who should banish the one who deserves to be banished. The people also agree to give a portion of their rice to the person whom they regard competent to perform these functions; the person so chosen accepts their offer keeping in view their common interest. In this way, the 'sovereign' comes into existence. In Buddhist literature, the 'sovereign' is described by three standing phrases: *Maha Sammata* (one who is chosen by the multitude); *Khattiya* (Sanskrit: *Kshatriya*) (one who is lord of the fields); and *Raja* (one who gratifies the others in accordance with *Dhamma)* (Gauba, 2015, pp. 33-34).

It is apparent from the *Aggañña Sutta* that the institution of government is an unfortunate necessity in an age of human degradation. When beings were closer to perfection and prior to the origination of the evil tendencies of greed and subsequently of private property among them, the society functioned without the need for a government. This implies that the Buddhists seemed to have preferred the stage of human evolution in which the evil passions of greed, pride, etc., and private property were non-existent. Conversely, the institution of government would not have become necessary if these evils – all of which arise from the notion of self – did not originate in the people. Therefore, we could conclude that the need for a government will cease to exist if and when the people become completely free from these evils, that is to say, when man reaches the state of selflessness (Dissanayake, 2009, p. 17).

The Buddha has refuted the *Brahmanic* theory based on the four-fold order of society which was claimed to be divine in origin and was, therefore, absolute. According to Buddhism, all irrespective of their social status or birth have equal rights and deserve to be treated equally. The fact that some of the so-called low born persons occupied some of the highest positions in the Order of the *Sangha* shows that everyone in the society deserves to have opportunities for the fullest development of his or her potentiality. The king of the Buddhist tradition being himself the fountain of justice should never deny any citizen of equality before the law.

The state is a sovereign entity and its sovereignty is expressed by a variety of terms. Sovereignty connotes total authority, an ability to reward and punish and capacity to give orders to all and receive orders from none. There were two major political systems in India in the sixth century B.C. when Buddhism emerged, namely Republician and Monarchical. Vajji, Malia and Sakya with which the Buddhist literature is familiar were republics and, Kosala and Magadha were among the best known and most powerful monarchies. The republics generally occupied the territory between the Ganges and the Himalayas and to the east of Kosala and the north-west of Magadha. These republics consisted of either a single tribe or a confederation of two, three or more tribes. The republics of the Mallas, the Licchavis, the Videhas and the Vajjis had formed themselves into a confederation. Usually a republic covered a small geographical area and each such republic had its own popular government run by an assembly of representatives and followed its own tribal customs and manners. The assemblies in which the political authority of the republics was vested were known as the *Sangha* or *Gana*. The representatives of the people who met in the City Hall to discuss matters of public interest and decide on state policy were usually of *Kshatriya* origin. However, others were not excluded. The person who presided over the assembly was called Raja. The office of the *Raja* was not hereditary and the person who occupied the position was a popular leader. Matters of public interest were discussed in the Assembly quite freely and decisions reached usually by consensus. If and when unanimity could not be reached the issue was put to a vote. The Assembly decisions were executed by a body of officials whose functions had been defined clearly. The collection of revenue, the army and the judiciary appear to be the most important among them (Gokhale, 1994, pp. 23-24).

It is conceivable that a legally established sovereign may lose the moral right to expect obedience from his subjects if he violates the commands of *Dhamma*. The early Buddhists added the concept of *Dhamma* to moralise the power of the state and transform it from being a legal institution into a moral force. Thus the early Buddhists envision the state as a pre-eminently moral institution equipped with coercive force the basis of which is not mere force of arms and capacity to use violence, but a moral constitution which endows it with an irresistible command (*ana*). Hence equipped, the state has the authority not only to impose ordinary law and order on the populace but also the right to guide the people in their moral endeavour. In this theory of *Dhamma* the *Brahmanical* theological sanctions have been largely eliminated and in their place is established the authority of a cosmic, supramundane mystic entity called *Dhamma*. *Dhamma* is expected to eliminate the violence, despotism, greed and arbitrariness inherent in the power of the state and make of it an instrument of higher morality. It constantly stands as a watchful guardian, in all its cosmic power and majesty, over the state, in all its actions protecting the subjects from the state and protecting the state against itself (Gokhale, 1994, p. 155).

References

Appadorai, A. (1992). Indian Political Thinking through the Ages. New Delhi: Khama Publishers.

Barua, D. K. (1971). An Analytical Study of Four Nikāyas. New Delhi: Munshiram Manoharlal Publishers Pvt. Ltd.

Dissanayake, P. (2009). Elementary Aspects of Buddhist Political Theory. Delhi: Critical Quest.

Dragonetti, F. T. (2013). Brahmanism & Buddhism: Two Antithetic Conceptions of Society in Ancient India. New Delhi: Critical Quest.

Gauba, O. (2015). Indian Political Thought. Indirapuram, UP: Mayur Paperbacks.

Gokhale, B. (1994). New Light on Early Buddhism. Bombay: Popular Prakashan.

Hackmann, H. and Theol, Lic. (1910). Buddhism as a Religion: Its Historical Development and Its Present Conditions. Delhi: Low Price Publications.

Murthy, D. K. (1991). A Dictionary of Buddhist Terms and Terminologies. Delhi: Sundeep Prakashan.

Prasad, B. (1974). Theory of Government in Ancient India. Allahabad: Central Book Depot.

Saletore, B. (1963). Ancient Indian Political Thought and Institutions. Bombay: Asia Publishing House.

Books for Further Reading

Appadorai, A. (1992). Indian Political Thinking through the Ages. New Delhi: Khama Publishers.

Bahuguna, Rameshwar Prasad, Dutta, Ranjeeta and Nasreen, Farhat (eds.) (2012). Negotiating Religion: Perspectives from Indian History. New Delhi: Manohar Publishers and Distributors.

Binod, Dr. Asha (2015). Bhagban Buddha: Buddha Dharma Ke Prabatraka. New Delhi: P.M. Publications.

Bose, Pramath Nath (--------). A History of Hindu Civilization during British Rule, Vol. 1. Delhi: Low Price Publications.

Carus, Paul (1961). The Gospel of Buddha, New Delhi: Director Publication Division. Ministry of Information and Broadcasting, Government of India.

Chakravarti, Ranabir (2016). Exploring Early India: UP to C.AD 1300. Third Edition. Delhi: Primus Books.

Collins, Steven (2001). Aggañña Sutta: The Discourse on What is Primary (An Annotated Translation from Pali). New Delhi: Sahitya Akademi.

Gokhale, Balkrishna D.Early Buddhist Kingship. The Journal of Asian Studies, Vol. XXVI, No.1, November 1966.

Jha, D.N. (2006). Ancient India: In Historical Outline. New Delhi: Manohar Publishers and Distributors.

Joshi, Lal Mani (2007). Brahmanism, Buddhism and Hinduism. New Delhi: Critical Quest.

Narula, Sanjay (2007). Ancient Indian Social and Political Thought. New Delhi: Murari Lal and Sons.

Sharma, L.P. (1981). History of Ancient India (Pre-historic Age to 1200 A.D.).

Sunita, Dr. (2014). Bharatiya Rajnitika Chintan. New Delhi: Kaberi Books.

Swaris, Nalin (2006). Buddhism, Human Rights and Social Renewal. New Delhi: Critical Quest.

Tyagi, Ruchi (2014). Prachinabam Madhyakalin Bharataka Rajnitika Chintan. Delhi: Hindi Madhyama Karyanaya Nirdeshalaya, Biswavidyalaya.

CHAPTER - FIVE

The Problem of Dīdārgañj Caurī Bearer's Identification- A Response

Kanika Gupta

In a paper published by Doris Meth Srinivasan, significant questions have been raised with respect to the identification of a monumental female sculpture in stone debatably dated to Mauryan period. Srinivasan proposes the identification of Dīdārgañj yakṣī with the royal courtesan, gaṇikā (Srinivasan 2005, 345-62). She begins with a discussion on textual references to gaṇikā from ancient and medieval periods which mainly refer to various gaṇikās, whether real or fictitious. The most prominent and closest to Mauryan period from these are Arthaśāstra, Kāmasūtra and Nāṭyaśāstra.

While beginning the discussion on images she states that sculptures with Mauryan polish are seen as those patronised by the Mauryan court. In this list she includes "the Pāṭaliputra caurī bearer". It is not quite clear if in these words she is referring to the Patnā yakṣa image, presently on display in Indian Museum Kolkata (Museum Accession Number P1). In fact, two such images are presently with Indian Museum Kolkata and they look almost the same. One of these is in reserve (Indian Museum Accession Number P2). Both are inscribed. Cunningham also talks about a third image which was being worshipped by the villagers when he saw it. Its present location is not known (Cunningham 1882, 2-3).

It should be pointed out that the Mauryan polish and its affiliation to royal patronage is a much-debated issue (Ray 1945, 48) and many scholars are of the view that this should not be connected with Mauryan patronage. So, even if Dīdārgañj yakṣī is dated to Mauryan period, this need not necessarily imply court patronage.

Her frontal stance and covered lower body have been considered by her as elements not seen often on yakṣī images. The presence of caurī is no doubt problematic to the extent that it makes the image subordinate. If Dīdārgañj image is to be placed in Mauryan period then it must be compared with other images which are debatably placed in this period. Few such images are two sculptures from Besnagar, one larger than life size and the other almost life size, yakṣī Lāyāva (Agrawala 1965, 118) from Mathurā and Parkham yakṣa (Cunningham 1882-83, 39-40; Quintanilla 2007, 26). The last two images of these from Mathurā have inscriptions and thus there is no doubt about their identification. The female image (yakṣī Lāyāva) is not a gaṇikā. Of course, she does not hold a caurī.

All of these images are frontal in pose with their body weight almost equally divided and their pudendum does not show. The smaller one from Besnagar holds something like corn or grain in her left hand (Vidiśā State Museum Accession No. 27; Fig. 1) which can be compared with a larger than life size image from Bharhut presently on display at Indian Museum Kolkata (Museum Accession No. 7 and 9; Fig. 2). What the Besnagar image holds in the other hand is not clear. Only a part of what looks like a handle is seen which could be a plant or a caurī. Though it is unlikely that it is a caurī, at least not like the one seen on Dīdārgañj image which is seen partly carved on the back of the image as well. Besnagar image's back shows no trace of a caurī. The other image from Besnagar, (Indian Museum Accession No. 1797; Fig. 3) has both her hands missing and her back too shows no trace of a caurī. A male image also from Besnagar holds a bag of money (Fig. 4) and there can be no doubt about identifying these images as those of yakṣa and yakṣī related to agriculture and wealth.

These images make it clear that frontal pose and non-visibility of pudendum were features of yakṣī and yakṣa images from Besnagar to be sure. Until this time showing the genital organs of these deities had not become a norm. The body weight of Dīdārgañj female is unequally placed on her legs according to Srinivasan. The present author however, is of the opinion that she stands equally on her two feet just like Besnagar images. Both her knees are slightly seen through her garment in the Besnagar fashion. This pose is also seen on many Bharhut images though not all[1] (Sirimā devata, Indian Museum Accession Number 141; Cunningham 1879, Plate XXIII). This frontal posture, with equal weight is seen carried forward in Indian sculpture at Sāñcī on nāga and nāgī images[2].

The most problematic element of the image, caurī, is also seen on the Patnā male image on display at Indian Museum Kolkata. This along with another image, exactly similar to the first one has been already discussed above. Both these men hold caurī in their hands and can be compared with the Dīdārgañj image. The present author is also of the opinion, that the female image too existed more in number just like the male images. But if the presence of caurī on the female image can make her secular then the same also has to hold good for the male images. The inscription on them goes against this supposition.

Patnā and Dīdārgañj Caurī Bearers Compared

Stylistic analysis remains one of the most important tools in the hands of an art historian which not only helps in appreciating the image but can also act as an evidence to trace movement of artist guilds. Significant work in this direction has been done by Misra (1975) and Kannal (1996). Professor Kannal employs this methodology towards tracing artistic lineages across the Indian subcontinent and through that throws fresh light on how artists worked and moved from one art centre to another. Attempts have been made to use the same methodology here while dealing with the style of images.

Out of the two yakṣa images found from Patnā, both presently with Indian Museum Kolkata, the one with its head lost is on display while the other which has its head intact though quite crude, is placed in reserve. The one without head has more portion of its body preserved thus enabling a better look at the approach of the artist. The torso or the upper portion of the sculpture is most life-like. Though Ray feels that the frontal portion of this sculpture is more naturalistic than its back (Ray 1945, 49), it is the opinion of the present author that it is the upper portion that appears more naturalistic to the contemporary eye. The lower portion appears, in comparison a bit more flat. The torso of this man along with whatever remains of his arms is almost human and the material quality of the stone has been left behind. The lower portion is more flat and the back of the waist garment along with the scarf (dupaṭṭā/uttariya hanging from the shoulder) almost act as a background surface on which a part of the image seems to rest. This flatness however, is much less if compared with Parkham yakṣa at Mathurā[3]. In front, even though a slight trace of the knees is seen, the overall treatment remains more flattish without highlighting any of the muscles of the legs.

What was held in the hand near the waist is not possible to tell, but the other raised hand held a caurī, an element also seen in the hand of Dīdārgañj yakṣī which has raised significant questions on the hierarchical position of the figures holding them. The other Patnā yakṣa is almost identical to the one discussed above which means that both had a caurī in their hands. It is possible that they were originally meant to be placed on either side of either a central image, or a human being (maybe king/ monarch) or a votive stūpa or a representative object of someone considered worthy of worship. In the same way, it is likely that another Dīdārgañj yakṣī existed which was placed in a similar manner which is either now lost to antiquity forever or maybe discovered in future. The mention of a third yakṣa image seen by Cunningham further suggests the possibility of multiple images of nature spirits used in a subordinate position. There are several other images in which secondary figures hold caurī to a central figure who is of primary significance in the depiction.

Thus, it should not be doubted that the presence of caurī in case of these images too shows their secondary position. What seems hard to believe is that such huge and larger than life size images should be made of characters who are of but secondary importance in a cult and nothing should be found of that which was the actual object of reverence. It must be kept in mind that these images belong to a period in which human representation was prohibited by the most popular cult of the time, namely – Buddhism. It is seen at Bharhut that life-size images of yakṣī, yakṣa and nāgarāja have been made in salutation to the central stūpa. Then it should not come as a surprise that these larger than life size images too were placed in salutation to something else.

The treatment of the lower body of Patnā images and Dīdārgañj image is similar. The drapes have been carved in the same fashion, the back side of the antariya touches the floor giving these images a royal look, and their frontal equally balanced weight with caurī held in one hand is sculpted in a similar way. All the three sculptures have Mauryan polish further confirming the probability (irrespective of their date)[4] that they were carved by sculptors belonging to the same local artist guild belonging to Pāṭaliputra region.

From the inscriptions at the back of the sculpture from Patnā and Parkham it is clear that image is that of a yakṣa. Yakṣa is depicted here as a wealthy strong man with only the caurī to place him in a subordinate position. Its absence would have qualified this image to the status of being independently worshipped due to the fact that not a single clue is available for its original context and its large size represents it as an image of someone quite important. He stands bare feet on something like a pedestal which is now mostly broken. The inscription is not written on this base, as is the case with Mathurā Parkham yakṣa. It is written on the dupaṭṭā/uttariya at the back of the image.

Issues of Identification

Regarding the connection between who is depicted and dating the image according to that identification, even if it is presumed without a single evidence that Dīdārgañj image is that of a gaṇikā, how does that help in dating it to Mauryan period? Gaṇikā existed in many cities in early historical period in the Indian subcontinent. Even if she is a gaṇikā from Pāṭaliputra, which period did she belong to and who or which king got her image made, this cannot be ascertained.

In Indian sculpture, the appearance of a fully developed sculpture in terms of skill, style and aesthetics is hardly a matter of surprise. This phenomenon is seen repeated several times in the entire history of Indian sculpture. Then why should the emergence of fully developed female and male images from present day Bihār region, without any precedents be seen as a surprise and completely impossible? The image can be assigned an early date on the grounds of its style and size; it can be placed within a larger date bracket due to the presence of Mauryan polish, but these conclusions cannot be drawn on the grounds of her identification with a gaṇikā. This is precisely what Srinivasan tries to do and her string of arguments and their various linkages must be reconsidered. Again, it must be agreed that her being a gaṇikā, cannot be conclusively denied just the way the reverse of it cannot be proved. Then how can another conclusion be drawn from something that itself remains a supposition and not a proven fact? A house of cards can be built only if the base is strong.

All the features of Dīdārgañj image help in stylistically placing it with others like her from Besnagar and Bharhut and there is no reason why these characteristics should not be associated with the cult of yakṣī worship. Here it must also be remembered that both Patnā yakṣa images in Indian Museum Kolkata are inscribed and the inscriptions can be paleographically dated to post Śuṅga period. One possibility is that the inscriptions were written in a later period since Dīdārgañj image is without one.

Srinivasan compares the Dīdārgañj image with one image only from Besnagar and few others from Mathurā. In her opinion Dīdārgañj image is different due to her uneven weight on her legs (which I do not agree with) and her caurī. In fact, the frontal pose and size are features which brings the Dīdārgañj image closer to the images mentioned by her instead of differentiating her from them. Following her argument, it is only the caurī that is different, a feature which is also seen on Patnā yakṣas. The biggest question now is that can the presence of caurī alone be considered an evidence strong enough to support her identification with a gaṇikā. Also, if caurī makes her a gaṇikā, what does a caurī make of the male images?

There is no doubt that Arthaśāstra (2.27.3) mentions caurī as a possession of a gaṇikā which she uses for the benefit of the king. The Candraketugarh panel is indeed striking in its similarity to the passage in the text (Shamasastry 1915, 244). In many sculptural panels as shown by Srinivasan one can see a king next to whom is a female figure with a caurī. But can all these female figures be a gaṇikā? Arthaśātra also refers to the king being always surrounded and protected by trusted women (Lahiri 2015, 55). Many of these women were warriors and would be armed according to the text. But can it be assumed that these texts were religiously followed by every monarch and its administration? There are other texts on similar lines like Kāmasūtra and Manusmriti. Were they also followed so strictly by the larger sections of population, monarchs and dynasties? A text is written based on social practices already prevalent in society and the ideology of the author shapes it; its prescriptions depend on what the author sees or would like his ideal society to be. Any text is necessarily selective in its choice of depicting social reality and at many places manipulates it to suit his agenda. Manusmriti prescribes inhuman punishments to women who transgress social and gender norms (8.370 – 8.371). Were all women who did transgress those boundaries punished in the prescribed manner? The fact that Manusmriti is so worried about maintaining a strict social order and is so severe in its punishments shows that there was quite a lot of transgression of those boundaries. Kāmasūtra's (3.11) author says in response to those who were of the opinion that Kāmaśāstra should not be taught to women, that people and women in their everyday lives practise skills like taming a horse, astrology and making love.

People do all this without necessarily referring to a text in their own way and therefore prohibiting a text to someone cannot stop someone from practising a certain skill. The purpose of his text therefore is to make the love life of people better, however, when in the actual act of making love, couples must do what comes to them naturally and what they think is best at that moment and not follow the written word in a compulsive manner. Similarly, Arthaśātra is a guidebook to make the control of a monarch over his state stronger and to ensure his safety better. It must not be assumed that it was adhered to strictly by one and all. Therefore, though the text says that a gaṇikā should have a caurī for the king and that she was employed by him, it must not be assumed that this actually happened at all points of time. Many kings are no doubt shown in sculpture with women around them. This does not necessarily imply that these women were gaṇikā. The position enjoyed by a gaṇikā varied. The example of Āmrapālī tell us that she enjoyed a powerful position in the town of Vaiśālī. She invites Buddha for a meal and it so happens that the Licchavis too want to invite Buddha at the same time. When they ask Āmrapālī to take her invitation back, she replies that even if they give her all their land (Vaiśālī) she would not agree to do so (Sanskritayan 1934, 237). Such a gaṇikā cannot be imagined with a caurī in her hand for the benefit of anyone. No doubt that Licchavis were a clan in the Vajji Janapada and Mauryans were monarchical rulers. In Arthaśāstra's ideal administration for a monarch, a gaṇikā must be employed by the state and abide by its law and serve the king with a caurī. But a text's ideal reality remains an ideal and cannot be taken to represent actual social practices and facts that might go against its will.

About the 'gracious bow' exhibited by Dīdārgañj image, it is, in fact hardly a bow; it is too subtle to be considered one and appears like a part of the female's personality and not as something she is purposely doing for a special occasion. An aesthetic interpretation of this slight bend of the female's back has been suggested by Professor Deepak Kannal[5]. He says that it is due to the heavy bosoms of the lady that her upper body is unable to take their weight and therefore slightly bends forward.

Regarding the identification of Bhājā sculpture, if it is indeed an image of Indra and Sūrya then it becomes the first of its kind and also the only one for a long time to come. However, an alternate and extremely convincing identification have been suggested by Deepak Kannal (Kannal 2005, 189) in which the two figures have been identified as historical kings. Srinivasan too would like to identify the Sūrya image as that of a king accompanied by gaṇikās. While it is true that a king is depicted along with women decked with jewellery it cannot be assumed that they are gaṇikā, someone who is not supposed to 'serve' only the king.

Kings in ancient India are also known for maintaining a harem and women in such a harem were not for people of the city at large but exclusively for the king. A king could be accompanied on his pompous processions by one his favourites from this harem as much as by a hired gaṇikā. To identify every bejewelled woman holding a caurī and accompanying a royal male figure as a gaṇikā would be over simplifying things. Arthaśāstra would like its gaṇikā to hold a caurī for its monarch but in reality, would every king be adamant on having the gaṇikā of his city hold a caurī for him? There is no evidence for such a norm anywhere except for the prescription of Arthaśāstra.

In light of the arguments presented above, Dīdārgañj female cannot be conclusively identified with a gaṇikā. Srinivasan suggests that the possibility of several such unidentified female figures being gaṇikā should remain open. Indeed, it should, but it must also be remembered that not a single female sculpture has yet been conclusively identified as a gaṇikā which is not the case with yakṣī images.

References

Agrawala, V.S. (1965). Studies in Indian Art. Varanasi: Vishwavidyalaya Prakashan.

Cunningham, Alexander (1879). The Stupa of Bharhut. London: W.H. Allen and Co..

Cunningham, Alexander (1882 – 83). Archaeological Survey of India Report, Vol. XX.

Cunningham, Alexander (1882) Report of a Tour in Bihar and Bengal in 1879-80. Calcutta: Archaeological Survey of India, Office of the Superintendent of Government Printing.

Dwivedi, Parasnath (trans.) (2014). Kamasutra. Varanasi: Chaukhamba Publishers, Reprint.

Kannal, Deepak (1996). Ellora: An Enigma in Sculptural Style. University of Michigan: Books & Books.

Lahiri, Nayanjot. (2015) Ashoka in Ancient India. New Delhi: Permanent Black.

Misra, R.N. (1975). Ancient Artists and Art-activity. Himachal Pradesh: Indian Institute of Advanced Studies.

Panikkar, Shivaji; Parul Dave Mukherji & Deeptha Achar (ed.) (2003). Towards a New Art History: Studies in Indian Art. Delhi: D.K. Printworld.

Quintanilla, Sonya (2007). History of Early Stone Sculpture at Mathura. Netherlands: Brill.

Ray, Niharranjan (1945). Maurya and Śuṅga Art. University of Calcutta.

Sanskritayan, Rahul (trans.) (1934). Vinaya Pitaka. Taiwan: The Corporate Body of the Buddha Educational Foundation, Taipei.

Shamasastry, R. (trans.) (2014). Kauṭilīya Arthaśāstra. Varanasi: Chowkhamba Vidyabhawan, , Reprint.

Journals

Srinivasan Doris Meth Srinivasan. "The Mauryan Gaṇikā from Dīdārgañj (Pāṭaliputra)". *East and West*, Vol. 55, No.1/4 (December 2005): 345-362. JSTOR accessed on 31 December 2017.

Endnotes

1 A larger than life-size image from Bharhut already mentioned, Indian Museum Accession Number 7, 9, also shares this feature.

2 Few sculptures of Nāga are at the site museum of Sāñcī and a nāgī image is in-situ.

3 With Parkham yakṣa, the discomfort of the artist while dealing with the sides of the image is quite clear. This stylistic analysis shows that the images created at Mathurā belong to a distinct local art tradition and those from Patnā, including Dīdārgañj image belong to a distinct school of sculpture making.

4 These sculptures could not have been carved more than a few decades away from each other.

5 Prof. Kannal has suggested this explanation in his lectures and unpublished papers several times at the Department of Art History and Aesthetics, Faculty of Fine Art, Maharaja Sayajirao University of Baroda, Vadodara, Gujarat.

CHAPTER - SIX

Gender Depiction in Visual Art

Apeksha Gandotra

With the passing away of historical time, the representations of history and behavior also changes. A process of engendering thus, takes place over a period of time. When conventions seem natural/ universal they are found to be more effective as we don't condition them in any way. For example, it is natural for a mother to take care of her own child.

A number of artists who were conventionally associated with the female nude are passed over in silence where as other work is considered, which is undoubtedly less familiar within the canon of art history. Anyone who examines the history of western art must be struck by prevalence of the female body. The female nude thus, connotes "Art" for them. The visual representation of the female nude body within the forms and frames of high art thus, depicts a discourse on the subject and is at the very center of the history of western aesthetics.

Even, social, and cultural representations are central in giving meaning to female body. Over the last decade, the notion that has gained popularity is that a women needs to be fit and thin; as being fat is excess, which needs to be done away with. As Michel Foucault[1] has shown that the body has become a highly politicized object, a site for display of power and control in the modern period. Thus, the women played out the roles of both viewed object and viewing object, forming and judging her image against cultural ideals and exercising a fearsome self-regulation. Even, Lynda Nead gives an example of the primacy of boundaries in social configuration of female body is anorexia nervosa. Here, again the body is seen as image, according to a set of conventions and women acts both as a judge and executioner. For the anorexic, there is always excess matter deposited over the surface of the body, which needs to be get ridden off.

Kenneth Clarks[2] in "The Nude" trace the history of the male and female nude from Greek antiquity to European modernism. Clark makes a distinction between the naked and the nude. It is a distinction between "bodies deprived of clothes" and "body clothed in art." The transformation from the naked to the nude is a shift from actual to the ideal that renders the nude the perfect subject for the work of art. As Clark states "The nude remains the most complete example of the transformation of matter into form". For Clark as Lynda Nead argues the category of the nude always holds within it a theory of representation. The nude is precisely the body in representation, the body produced by culture. John Berger, on the other hand argues that whereas the nude is always subjected to pictorial conventions, "To be naked" he writes, is "to be oneself". To be naked is thus, to be free of patriarchal conventions of western society. For Berger hence, naked is now the positive term and the nude is relegated to the inferior position within the opposition.

T.J. Clark[3] in his reading of Manet's painting Olympia in 1865, draws on a more complex reworking of the naked/nude dichotomy. He defines nude as "a picture for men to look at, in which women is constructed as an object of somebody else's desire". Nakedness for Clark, is a mark of material reality, whereas nudity transcends the historical and social existence and is a kind of cultural disguise. Although the naked and nude are no longer structured within an oppositional pairing, they still represent a greater and a lesser degree of cultural mediation, with nakedness still representing the more transparent signs of class and sexuality.

If the female nude is understood discursively, not only as a set of images but in terms of its formation through institutions such as schools, galleries, publishing houses, then the concept of tradition is helpful in knowing the cultural power of the discourse. The projection of female nude in a high range of images is attributed to the skill of Titian, Rubens, Boucher, Manet and Picasso – with variations in depicting various artistically rich tendencies. Laura Mulvey[4] in "Visual pleasure and Narrative cinema" argues that the image of women as (passive) raw material for the active gaze of man shows the ideology of the patriarchal order in its favorite cinematic form –narrative film. Cinema thus, shapes the way a women is to be looked at into the spectacle itself. The camera becomes the mechanism for providing an illusion of Renaissance space, flowing movements compatible with human eye to create a convincing world. In explaining gender constructs in visual art, Seema Bawa in "Gods, men and women" talks of a paradox as on one hand our society revers goddesses while on the other hand the same society disregards women's rights. By focusing on the art of the post-mauryan period, she examines women different representations such as wives, non-wives, ogresses, mothers, married couples etc. For example, she examines "Lajja-Gauri" and "Dugdhadharini" as exhibiting reproductive qualities. She poses a question as to whether representation of reproductive qualities by showing genitilia and breasts represent female reproductive power or does it reduce women to their reproductive function alone.

Bawa uses Judith Butler's work on gender as performance to recognize markers of gender in outward manifestations such as postures, clothes and jewelry. By reading silences she tries to unravel the power structures. For instance, Maya Devi, mother of Buddha is shown standing while giving birth rather than lying down which Bawa posits could be a negative attitude towards women's sexuality; thus, depicting suffering during child birth.

Conclusion

Thus, it can be concluded that representation of the female body is at the center of feminist cultural politics and women artists are using images of the female body in order to make visible a range of female identities. For feminists to reclaim the female body means to challenge the authority of patriarchal boundaries- boundaries of gender and identity and between art and obscenity. It is an ongoing struggle, but with the increasing role of media and growth of a wider audience there will be more spaces opening out for feminist voices to be heard and for female images to be seen.

References

Bawa, Seema (2013). Gods, Men and Women: Gender and Sexuality in Early Indian Art. New Delhi: D.K. Print world.

Clark, Kenneth (1956). The Nude: A Study of Ideal Art. London: John Murray, pp.79.

Clark, T.J. (1980). Preliminaries to a Possible Treatment of Olympia in 1865. Screen, 21:1. Spring, pp. 18 – 41.

Foucault, Michel (1981). The History of Sexuality: An Introduction, translated by Robert Hurley. Volume 1 Harmondsworth: Penguin.

Marley, Laura (1975). Visual Pleasure and Narrative cinema. Screen Autumn 1975, Vol. 16, No. 3, pp. 6-18.

Nead, Lynda (1992). The Female Nude (Art, Obscenity and Sexuality). New York: Routledge.

Endnotes

1 Foucault, Michel (1981). The History of Sexuality: An Introduction Trans. by Robert Hurley, Volume 1. Harmondsworth: Penguin.

2 Clark, Kenneth (1956), The Nude: A Study of Ideal Art. London: John Murray.

3 Clark, T.J. (1980), Preliminaries to a Possible Treatment of Olympia in 1865. Spring, pp. 18-41.

4 Mulvey Laura, "Visual Pleasure and Narrative Cinema", Screen Autumn 1975, Vol. 16 No. 3 , pp 6-18.

Section – II
Medieval History

CHAPTER - SEVEN

The Interconnection between History and Literature

Vandana Rana

The practice of history writing doesn't take place in isolation. It gets influenced by the material culture in which it is written. Thus, one can't deny the relation between history and culture. The evaluation of the nature and function of the process of history writing allow us to look into the cultural, social as well as political spheres of that period. As far as "culture" is concerned there is hardly any disapproval that literature forms an integral part of culture. Popular experiences are generally expressed through the medium of literature. Literature is able to penetrate in those areas where the modern discipline of history writing based on European principles, generally can't. What is needed is to redefine the whole concept of history writing.

The scope of "history" should be widened and it should not only focus on state centered sources such as archives, chronicles etc. In fact, accounts of common people should also be given preference by focusing on vernacular histories and literary accounts, as argued by Partha Chatterjee. Not only this but certain historical narratives written in literary forms in the early modern period of Indian history fulfils all the conditions of modern historiography but still not treated as historical accounts. Moreover, one should also critically evaluate how certain texts are put in the category of "history" while the others are treated as mere fictional accounts. Kumkum Chatterjee has discussed this issue in her work. The politics behind this deliberate categorization should not be ignored. The idea of treating history as a scientific, rational and objective discipline is a modern construct. One should understand the earlier modes of relating to the past in its own terms in which various kinds of literary forms played a crucial role. C. A. Bayly has argued in the same line when he wrote that the process of Indo-Persian history writing of the eighteenth century has a distinct "Indian Acumen". Similarly, V. Narayan Rao, David Shulman and Sanjay Subramaniyam have also explored the field of history writing during eighteenth century in the context of Indian subcontinent. Thus, this essay will try to throw some light over these issues and will explore the interconnection between history and literature.

To know the linkage between history and literature it is important to know how this distinction was made between factual and fictitious accounts. What classifies a text as a "literary text" or a piece of history? What are the qualities which are associated with literature and history? The modern concept of history as a rational and scientific discipline, can be traced back to nineteenth century Europe where it is seen as a medium to explore "past realities" on the basis of verifiable evidence, studied objectively. This concept of history narrowed the domain of this discipline. It excluded all those modes of remembering the past, from the category of history, which do not fit in this definition. Thus, this classified many societies as "Ahistorical" before the arrival of Europeans such as South Asia, Africa and Latin America, where the accounts remembering the past are not considered as historical texts. These areas, hence, according to the European observers, had no tradition of history writing. When British colonial rule was established in India then many British writers such as James Mill, Thomas Babington Macaulay etc. expressed disdain about the inability of Indians to write proper history.

But as Kumkum Chatterjee has argued that it is true that

the British colonial rule brought a new way of history writing to Indian subcontinent but then it can't be automatically assumed that pre-modern India did not have a historical consciousness. History writing in pre-modern India was not a specialized practice associated with formal institutions. As Romila Thapar noted that 'it was a practice which was "embedded" in various kinds of narratives, thereby sometimes tendering it difficult for modern readers, accustomed to regarding history as a self-contained "exclusive" discipline, to identify in a material which defied such characterization (Romila Thapar, Society and Historical Consciousness: The Itihas-Purana Tradition). The modern definition of history, seeing it as rational positivist discipline, fails to recognize the various modes of writing history in pre-modern India when literary forms like "kavya", use verses instead of prose as a means to write history. This pre-modern historiography is seen by European scholars as lacking a proper methodology and distinction between what is factual and fictional. In contrast to this V. Narayan Rao, David Shulman and Sanjay Subramaniyam have argued that the audience of that time was able to distinguish between factual and fictional details by the mere texture of the narrative which included different kinds of textual markers. So, it is necessary to view pre-modern means of history writing with a different perspective.

The various pre-modern texts which remember the past can be broadly put into two categories, one which fulfils all the conditions of modern historiography but still does not get a place within the category of "history" and second, those text which do not confirm the various modern features associated with history writing but still can prove to be an important text in the context of commemorating the past. Rao-Shulman-Subramaniyam has shown that there are narratives of the pre-modern time which are based on facts and focuses the state and informs about the credibility of the sources and also bound by secular causal explanation but such narratives come from non-historical literary genres like poems, ballads or from the itihas-purana traditions.

Yet these narratives were considered by their readers or listeners as historical narratives. So, the argument of Rao-Shulman-Subramaniyam is that if history is defined by its modern definition as rational discipline based on verifiable evidences then this tradition of history writing was present in India much before the arrival of the British.

There is no dearth of texts which can be put in the above mentioned first category, for instance, Prachi Deshpande has discussed the distinct tradition of *Bakhar* writing which recorded history of a lineage or of a family of property or political distinction or of significant events, in the western part of India, in the Marathi speaking region. She has shown how *Bakhar* placed events in a sequence and showed why and how they happened through a literary recreation of the past. Sumit Guha has also highlighted that *Bakhar* emerged as local factual narratives and he viewed their literary and historical qualities together rather than separating them. Apart from this Rao-Shulman-Subramaniyam also saw the *Mangal Kavya* tradition of Bengal as a historical narrative formed in a different literary genre. David L. Curley also saw the *Mangal Kavya* as a source which provides a window to political, social, economic and social conflicts of that period.

Partha Chatterjee has shown how vernacular texts are put in the category of literature despite of the fact that they were considered by the contemporary audience as historical narratives. In this regard he has given a series of examples. For instance, he showed how in north-eastern India particularly in Assam, *Buranji* tradition became a source of writing history in pre-colonial Assam. Yasmin Saikia points out that the first evidence of a *Buranji* comes from the seventeenth century but she says it was a distinct pre-colonial tradition of writing history, very different from the Indo-Persian style which already existed at that time.

Moreover, how certain themes and tradition got transformed with the coming of the colonial rule is also necessary to explore. Rao and Subramaniyam have identified one such history writing tradition, that is, the *niti* tradition written in Telugu. These texts which appeared between fifteenth and seventeenth century in southern India were considered distinct from dharma and can be considered as historical accounts on the basis of modern definition of history. But in the nineteenth century these *niti* tradition were confused with 'moral instructions' and were ultimately replaced. Even the nationalist thinkers of the late nineteenth century rejected *niti* tradition as ignoble aspect of India's past. This explains how certain historical accounts in various literary genres which could give valuable information gradually phases out.

Partha Chatterjee has argued that is it correct to dismiss the vernacular historical accounts and different literary genres just because they do not confirm with the principles of western academic history writing practices. According to him, they do have an equally valid claim to be rational historiographic practices. He has also pointed out these genres offer us a richer account of the true history of the people. It gives us the account of those who have witnessed historical changes themselves. These vernacular histories exposes the relation between literature and history. It shows how these histories which are no doubt different from the western academic histories, use different literary genres like verses, poems, novels, drama etc. to recreate the past event. It is true that these accounts may have fictionalized past events but here it is important to note that these texts are not known for the historical truth which can be verified scientifically rather these text serve a far more important purpose as they give us an account from inside, they tell us about the experiences of people. So, one can say that these narratives enrich our historical knowledge.

Since, as it is already shown by Partha Chattaerjee, Rao-Shulman-Subramaniyam, Kumkum Chatterjee and others that India did not lack a historical consciousness in the pre-colonial period, one could focus on how the study of different literary genres in which these historical accounts were written, can give us a glimpse of the culture, society and even polity of that period. The practice of history writing is such that it can never take place in isolation. It gets influenced by the prevailing culture and political scenario. In pre-colonial India often the historical texts were written in only that language which represented the political elite class of that time. Thus, before the Turkish invasion it was more or less Sanskrit and in the Mughal period Persian became dominant. By studying the literary style adopted by these accounts one could trace how culture and political set ups changed throughout history.

Kumkum Chatterjee in her work *The Cultures of History in Early Modern India: Persianization and Mughal Culture in Bengal* has explored that how the practice of history writing during the early modern period was influenced by the prevailing Persian culture. According to her, history writing in the early modern period was not about repeating unchanging notions of the past rather 'it served as political and cultural statements derived from their immediate environments'. She showed that though historiographical narratives during the seventeenth and eighteenth centuries in Bengal were primarily written in Sanskrit or in Bengali but during this period they displayed a remarkable shift in terms of content and idioms. These new elements were drawn from the Persian language.

During this time Persian tarikhs were also written, this also indicate the growing importance of Persian as a language. The study of the content of these historical narratives not only tell us about the cultural sphere of that time but also show who was politically dominant. Muzaffar Alam has shown how Persian language was closely associated with Mughal governance. The influence of Persian over Sanskrit and vernacular texts as well as the increasing number of tarikh tradition tell us a lot about the growing political power of Mughals. Kumkum Chatterjee has argued that how the provincial aristocracy of Bengal gradually accepted the aspects of this Persianized tradition. This indicates towards the reception and acceptability of Mughal rule by its subjects. Thus, only through a mere study of language used in historical narratives can give us information about the political culture of that period. This gives us yet another connection between history and literature.

Allison Busch in his essay 'Literary Responses to the Mughal Imperium: The Historical Poems of Kesavdas' has tried to integrate both literary and historical traditions. He has focused mainly on three works of Kesavdas- *Ratnabavani, Virsimhdevacarita, and Jahangirjascandrika*. The first is a short narrative poem highlighting the valor of Orcha king Ratansena while fighting with the Mughal emperor Akbar. The next is a chronicle of Ratansena's brother Bir Singh Bundela who is seen as the most powerful ruler of the Orcha dynasty. The third is a collection of praise poems written for the Mughal emperor Jahangir. As with the coming of Mughals, Persian became dominant, similarly the political events related to Orcha dynasty influenced the writings of Kesavdas. These text give us a glimpse of how relation between Orcha and Mughal Empire underwent changes over a period of time. In the first work, *bavani*, Mughals are frequently referred as Mlechhas and it showed how Akbar's reign provoked hatred towards the Mughals among the people of Orcha but in the second text, that is, *Virsimhdevcarit*, the term Mlechha got completely vanished and in the third text Kesavdas compared the Mughal emperor, Jahangir, to Hindu god-kings like Rama and Indra.

Busch also tried to show how sometimes the distinction between history and literature does not seem much meaningful. For this he has illustrated how both Kesavdas in his *Carit* and Jahangir in his autobiographical account *Jahangirnama* mention the murder of Abul Fazl without giving much details. Moreover, both acknowledged the noble qualities of Abul Fazl and the grief of the Mughal emperor Akbar. But Kesavdas' text is generally kept in the category of untrustworthy 'Hindu Lore' where as *Jahangirnama* ranks high on the truth scale. Despite of adopting different literary strategies there is similarity in both the texts and this shows that sometimes the line between history and literature blurs.

Another important point which is highlighted by Busch is that we as modern readers take the *riti* tradition on its face value. We fail to understand the inherent meaning hidden behind that ornate language. One should try to understand the original performative meaning of these texts. For instance, every quality of Bir Singh Bundela projects him as a ruler who is fit to rule and this fitness to rule is measured by the grandeur of the text. The two reinforce each other.

Through the study of these three historical poems of Kesavdas, Allison Busch has argued that 'the fictive and factual domains do not conflict in the text rather they intersect and enrich each other'. The literary style adopted by Kesavdas was his "choice", a choice made by an agent of culture at a particular point of time and thus it tells us a lot about the cultural sphere of that period and helps to reconstruct the past of that period. Moreover, according to him, Poetry offers a historian a richer perspective of the past. It does not try to locate a single truth rather it shows how different versions compete with each other for their claim to truth. He says that 'poetry's fictionality has its own truth, regardless of its factuality'. So, a historian can use these poetic tradition to reconstruct the past in a better way and instead of seeing literature and history as two distinct and contrary spheres one should study them in a more integrating manner.

Thus, the scope of history as a discipline should be widened. It should also acknowledge historical narratives written in different literary genres and also vernacular histories that do not strictly follow the principles of academic history writing. The earlier modes of relating to the past should be understood in the context of that period. In the pre-modern time literary forms were generally used to write historical accounts but European observers relegated those accounts to the category of fictions and declared that Indian subcontinent lacked historical consciousness during the pre-modern time. They were trying to locate historical texts based on modern principles in the pre-modern time. By acknowledging various literary genres and vernacular histories such as *mangal kavyas, bakhars, buranji tradition, riti tradition* etc. one could get a better and more nuanced understanding of the past.

References

Busch, Allison (2005). Literary Responses to the Mughal Imperialism: The Historical Poems of Kesav Das. New Delhi: Sage Publications.

Curley, David L. (2008). Poetry and History: Bengali Mangal-Kabya and Social Change in Precolonial Bengal. Kerala: D.C. Publishers.

Chatterjee, Kumkum (2009). The Culture of History in Early Modern India: Persianization and Mughal Culture in Bengal. Oxford: Oxford University Press.

Chatterjee, Partha (2008). History in the Vernacular. New Delhi: Permanent Black.

Deshpande, Prachi (2007). Creative Pasts: Historical Memory and Identity in Western India 1700-1960. New Delhi: Orient Blackswan.

Thapar, Romila; Society and Historical Consciousness: The Itihasa- Purana Tradition

CHAPTER - EIGHT

Understanding the Rise of Mongol Military Power and its Implications on Research

TCA Achintya

The emergence of the Great Khaganate under Genghis Khan represents one of the fastest rises to power of any polity recorded in History. Genghis Khan, in the span of a single lifetime, united the disparate Central Asian tribes which were broadly considered Mongol, and then proceed to conquer swathes of territory controlled by some of the premier world powers of the era. Genghis' rags to riches story would perhaps appear a fantasy if it had not been so well recorded in the histories of so many cultures. This was a man who, along with his family, had been reduced to penury and cast out into the wilderness following the death of his father. And yet, he managed to rise to power, reclaiming authority not just within the political structures of the tribal culture of the nomadic Mongols, but redefined the system itself, forging a new nation where previously there had been none, and creating a military powerhouse that would reshape the political boundaries of Asia, leaving an indelible mark on the people it encountered.

What was it about the Mongols that allowed them to rise so rapidly to power in such a large area? Part of the answer to this lies, of course, in understanding the political scenario of the world as it existed. The Mongols were adept at exploiting political differences between regional powers. Their conquests of the Tangut kingdom (also called the Xi-Xia), the Jurchens, and the Khwarazm dynasty, were all accomplished at least in part through exploiting diplomatic conditions and ensuring they did not face an enemy which was diplomatically well supported by allies, thus making sure that their opponent stood alone rather than part of a formidable coalition. But Mongol military skills and tactics also go into explaining why the Mongols became such an overwhelming force in the days of the Great Khagans. It therefore becomes important to understand the nature of the Mongol military machine and how it stood apart, to gain insight into the rapidity and depth of their conquests.

To understand the prowess of the Mongols first and foremost requires the busting of a few popular notions that exist concerning the Mongol conquest. First is the myth that the Mongols succeeded because they possessed technological superiority over contemporary armies, and that their nomadic methods and predominantly cavalry and archery based forms of warfare had been heretofore unseen, thus allowing them to triumph in the early decades before other powers "adapted" to these new strategies. This myth is relatively easy to negate, given its weak evidentiary support and lack of corroboration. The first thing to understand here is that the Mongol style of warfare was hardly new to the world. Armies of predominantly cavalry archers and fighters and of nomadic groups with higher mobility and military traction had been around since the early Ancient Period. The Ancient Scythians had preyed upon armies from Greece to India. The Achaemenid Persian Empire had employed entire corps of horse archers to deadly effect as early on as the 6th century BC. Nomadic, horse archer and cavalry centric forces had been at the core of invading peoples such as the Huns, Cumans and Xiongnu in India, Europe and China. Thus, the armies of these regions had a long history of contact with nomadic cavalry centric armies and a record of several successes (alongside periods of failures), dating to the period of the Roman Empire in Europe, the Gupta Empire in India and the Han Dynasty in China. The basic tactics employed by the Mongols were hardly a radical innovation, and contrary to lay perceptions do not represent the sort of advantage over their contemporaries that the Spanish Conquistadors or Dutch Commandos enjoyed with gunpowder over the natives of Latin America or Southern Africa. While it is true that the later Mongols were quick to adopt gunpowder technology, its efficacy in the battlefield was initially quite limited (if not counter-productive). Moreover, the incorporation of gunpowder cannot explain the conquests of Genghis or Ogedei, which occurred before the Mongols had gunpowder weapons.

The second notion is a little more complicated, namely that of the numbers involved in the Mongol conquests. The arrival of the Mongols was met with a deep sense of shock and despair by the Europeans and Muslims at the overwhelming power and speed of the conquests of what were, to them, essentially a race of wild barbarians. We can judge the extent of this by looking at our notion of the Mongol "Horde", derived from the Mongolian "Ordu". The imagery of the Mongol armies is that of a vast swarm of wild barbaric soldiers sweeping over tiny organized armies of civilized nations and destroying all in their path. This image is based at least in part on contemporary Islamic sources, some of which insist that the Mongols greatly outnumbered their enemies in the invasions of the Khwarazm Empire. However, this notion is certainly factually inaccurate when describing the vast majority of Mongol conquests in China and Europe, especially during the early phase of their conquests. The Mongols were outnumbered 20,000 to 30,000 against the Kara-Khitai; 30,000 to 270,000 against the Xi-Xia; 100,000-120,000 to anywhere between 500,000-1,000,000 against the Jurchen (though the Jurchen numbers are believed to have been heavily exaggerated and likely conflated soldiers with supporting non-combatants)[1]. In Europe, according to both traditional and revised numbers, they were inevitably outnumbered by a ratio of some 3-1 or more in their raids/conquests. The niggling issue is therefore that of Central Asia, specifically that of the Khwarazm Empire. Historians such as David Morgan, John France and Denis

Sinor have instead argued that contrary to the sources of the time, the Mongols were outnumbered by the Shah of Khwarazm. This is broadly based on looking at the work of Rashid-al-Din Hamadani, in conjunction with logistical analyses and comparisons to other Mongol campaigns. Other historians nonetheless have disagreed[2] with this assessment. Regardless of which side we take in this facet of the broader history of Mongol conquests, it is undeniable that in general the Mongols faced enemies with either numerical (at times vastly so) inferiority or parity and yet triumphed, often quite comprehensively. And many of these battles were not against poorly equipped or led armies but the cream of the medieval era. The armies of Europe comprised elite forces such as the Templar and Teutonic order of Knights fighting alongside the Hungarian and Russian forces. In China, the Mongol Tumens faced the Jin, Song and Xi-Xia dynasties.

We therefore see that the idea of the Mongol "horde" is misplaced. These were not vast armies sweeping all that stood before them. Instead they were small forces, defeating well equipped, larger or comparable forces in battle after battle. The key to understanding the Mongol armies thus lies in understanding the things that allowed them to stand apart. First, let's consider the technological. The Mongol compound bow was certainly an excellent example of military engineering. Despite being a smaller cavalry bow, it outraged the contemporaneous English longbow (widely acknowledged across the medieval world as having the longest range) by almost 100 meters[3]. This gave the Mongols an advantage over other armies that traditional cavalry-archer forces had not enjoyed[4] in the past. But this is not enough to explain the superiority of the Mongol armies.

Another issue which gave them an edge was the structure of Mongol society which, due to its nomadic and semi agro-pastoral nature, gave them significant mobility and speed. They had the ability to cover as much as 160 kilometer in a single day. Enhancing their speed and strategic mobility was the fact that the Mongol cavalryman in general travelled with some 3-4 remounts[5]. This, combined with the known stamina and speed of the Mongolian Pony[6], gave the Mongol armies unprecedented speed.

Genghis' greatest innovation was the restructuring of the traditional nomadic army into a strictly organized hierarchical structure, based on decimal units, the smallest being 10 men, up to discrete armies of 10,000. The Mongol armies, as historians have demonstrated, were highly disciplined and well trained, while retaining flexibility and autonomy in command and control. The Italian explorer Giovanni da Pian del Caprine noted "The Tartars—that is, the Mongols—are the most obedient people in the world in regard to their leaders, more so even than our own clergy to their superiors."[7]. Transfers between units were forbidden. The leaders on each level had significant license to execute their orders in the way they considered best. This command structure proved to be highly flexible and allowed the Mongol army to attack en-masse, divide into somewhat smaller groups to encircle and lead enemies into an ambush, or divide into small groups of as little as 10 for mop up operations. Individual soldiers were responsible for their equipment, weapons, and up to five mounts, although they fought as part of a unit. Their families and herds would accompany them on foreign expeditions, although usually at a distance, in the case of initial forays into enemy territory[8].

Thus, the Mongol army, enormously disciplined, flexible, and fast, with a strong strategic mix of heavy and light troopers, was definitely not an unorganized "horde"[9]. It was a powerful, organized, and well led military machine. The Mongol Army of the Great Khaganate can be held to the same standards as the armies of the Roman Republic/Empire or Alexander the Great - armies which have been extolled by Western scholars and amateur historians alike as being among the best military forces in the world. The Mongol army certainly meets the very same checklist which sets apart the forces of Ancient Rome and Macedon. Like these great armies, the Mongols enjoyed the use of a unique weapon engineered to suit their style of combat and generally superior to other similar tools in use at the time (comparable to the Roman pilum and gladius and the Macedonian sarissa). They were highly disciplined, had clear and flexible hierarchies of command[10].

Lastly, let us look at leadership. Almost everyone in the world has heard of Alexander the Great's Macedonian Empire and Julius Caesar under the Republic. Anyone associated with the field of history has no doubt heard of associated subordinate generals, instrumental in their success. Historians know that for Alexander, it was Parmenion, Cleitus, Ptolemy or Antigonus; in Rome it was generals such as Pompey, Gaius Marius, and Lucullus. Yet few would be aware of names such as Jelme, Jebe or Subutai. Genghis' reputation has been built up in popular perception more as a barbarian warlord than a general whose achievements and genius arguably outstrip those of Caesar or Alexander. Even the achievements of his subordinates such as Subutai outclassed the conquests of the great heroes of Western Civilization.

As we should be able to observe, in nearly every parameter of comparison, the institution that was the Mongol Army ranks amidst the finest known to history. The Legions of Rome, the Phalanxes of Macedon and the Armies of the British Empire - the Mongols are as good as any of them. It is this knowledge that helps provide an answer to understanding the conquests of the Mongols. They did not carve the largest pre-modern empire known to Man because they were wild untamed barbarians, nor because they faced weak or corrupted enemies who easily fell prey to them. The Mongol war machine was a finely tuned organization that succeeded because of the skills it had perfected. As military powers go, despite their nomadic nature, and despite their predominantly cavalry centric approach, the Mongols, and leaders such as Genghis Khan or Ogedei, were on par, if not superior to, the likes of Alexander or Caesar. It is worth noting that Alexander's conquests fell apart almost as soon as he died, whereas Genghis' conquests not only survived well after his death, but left a political legacy of enormous magnitude. The institution of the Khagan remained powerful for nearly a century after Genghis established his power, and even in its decline, it was succeeded by political institutions which also had their roots in Mongol culture. The powerful states of the Ilkhanate, the Yuan dynasty, and the Golden Horde all lasted for many decades. In pure military terms the Mongols, and specifically Genghis Khan, were arguably more successful than any of the western "Greats". It is therefore time that we begin to reconsider the role and respect that we grant to Genghis and his generals when discussing our history.

However, one natural question that might flow from this discourse on Mongol superiority is this: If the Mongol Armies rested on such a strong foundation of military strength, why did they suffer such drastic strategic reversals during the time of the later Khagans such as Mongke or Kublai? The answer lies in understanding the basics of Mongol society. The Mongols were fundamentally a nomadic culture. Unlike the sedentary cultures of Greece and Rome, their overall population numbers were never very high. Over time, therefore, their ability to replenish numbers reduced drastically. Specific Mongol traditions of concentrating resources with the youngest also had the impact of removing the core of Genghis' "Mongol" army from the successor states such as Jochi's Golden Horde, the Chagatai Khanate, The Ilkhanate and the Yuan dynasty.

Finally, it is important to recognize that aspects of their strength were also the cause of their weakness - their adaptability. The Mongols, like many of the greatest armies of history, were quick to adapt technologies and fighting styles which they found advantageous and could be utilized in conjunction with their own tactics. Thus, just as the Romans famously adapted the shield and sword tactics of the Illyrians, or absorbed auxiliary infantry, archers and cavalry from conquered subjects, the Mongols are notable for adapting gunpowder to their military needs, and for adapting local armies such as the Chinese Pike units into their structures. As the empire expanded, however, this led to inundation. As the Mongolians were culturally inundated, with Islamic culture taking over the Ilkhanate and Golden Horde, and Chinese-

Buddhist culture taking over the Yuan, their military structures also got inundated. The succession pattern established by Genghis concentrated the bulk of the traditional Mongolian Tumens with Tolui in the traditional homeland. The result of these policies and actions was that very quickly the armies of the Mongolian states in China and Central Asia become largely composed of soldiers and fighting styles recruited from the local regions, with only a small, often tiny, core of the old style Mongol troops. The armies which would face strategic reversals in Europe, in West Asia such as Ain Jalut, and the disastrous campaigns in Vietnam and Japan, were therefore composed of only a small fraction of the deadly units which were instrumental in the success of Genghis. The reason for the seemingly sudden and drastic reversals was not just due to the local armies getting "used" to Mongol tactics and strategies, but equally due to the quality of the Mongol armies in the successor states being severely diluted and significantly altered from its traditional origin. Meanwhile, the introduction of cannons, the greater dependency on infantry, and the shift from self-sustaining and heavily remounted armies, to city dependent supply lines and support systems transformed the fast and agile Mongol Tumens into far more ponderous and lumbering institutions. Broadly speaking, the Mongols were unable to maintain the institutions which had been the cause of their rapid successes.

When we compare the Mongols to empires such as the Romans and Greeks, it is important to not get carried away, however. It should be kept in mind that the essence of my comparison lies in comparing military structures and the influence of society in the context of the military. The analysis that the Mongols have been misunderstood insofar as military matters go, should not be seen as a brief for them. That the military abilities and achievements of the Mongols were innately superior to that of Alexander, does not imply that their cultural contributions were also equal. The mistake many historians make is that in seeking to rehabilitate the image of the Mongols on issues where the evidence supports such rehabilitation, they go overboard to the other extreme, ending up trying to whitewash their actions altogether[11]. The Mongols were destroyers par excellence, and the demographic and cultural damage done by Genghis and his successors is felt even to this day. The Mongol conquest of Mesopotamia, specifically Baghdad, under Hulegu Khan is an excellent example of this. The destruction wrought by this successor of Genghis was so complete that it transformed a region which had been among the wealthiest in the world into one of utter backwardness. Where once the Babylonian culture flourished, being one of the greatest centres of knowledge and wealth, Hulegu left behind a wasteland. The damage done by Hulegu to the irrigation system of Mesopotamia, which had flourished for thousands of years and helped sustain a vast population, was so permanent, that the region was depopulated and suffered repeated invasions over the centuries, eventually causing a breakdown of social and economic order that plagues the region to this day[12]. Understanding the reasons for this damage is key to gaining insight into the Mongols. As historians, it is important to not fall into the trap of letting morality dictate conclusions on subject matter. The actions of the Mongols were not motivated by an intrinsic disdain for morality, nor were the Mongols as a people any more or less capable of violence than their contemporaries. The reality is that the Mongols, particularly the governing elite, came from a cultural background that had strong roots in nomadic culture. While Genghis and his sons grew up in the culture itself, his later successors were also strongly influenced by these aspects of their life. The early Mongols therefore, as nomads, did not share the same respect for the institutions and structures that sedentary peoples possessed. The differences in these attitudes, in my opinion, flowed from a basic dissonance in notions of property, with the nomadic Mongols holding extremely different notions of what was property and what held value. To them, land was meaningless; property was how many horses or how many heads of cattle one owned; whereas for sedentary people, value and wealth flowed essentially from land. The Mongols held little value for the institutions that flowed from this respect of land. Conversely, one should not make the assumption that the Mongols as a people held no respect for learning, scholarship, or other cultural features. They were instrumental in stabilizing the silk route which, since the collapse of the Sassanid dynasty, had fallen into disuse in the fractured and unstable political landscape of Asia. Similarly, the Mongols are famous for their "secularism" or tolerance of the multiplicity of faiths within their kingdoms. Mongol cities such as Karakorum were notable for the synthesis of cultures and as a meeting ground for people of various backgrounds, and may well have played a role in the flowering of new cultural patterns in Persian and Chinese literature that took place under their rule. The Mongol power therefore represents a unique historical phenomenon to historians, and one which must be understood with care. Very rarely has a nomadic power successfully established a large political base in recorded history, before merging with established sedentary patterns. Cultures such as the Huns and Scythians come to mind. The Mongols are among the ones with the greatest historical record however (though even so, it is much less than what we find for contemporary sedentary cultures). Recognizing these differences is important in constructing an adequate articulation of the role played by Mongols in History.

The last aspect I seek to explore with this paper is therefore the potential for research. One feature which has always fascinated me about the Mongols is the power of women in elite politics. Among the nobility of the Mongols we find an interesting phenomenon. In the interregnum that existed between the death of a Khagan and the election of a new Khagan by the Qurultai, we find that the wife of the Khagan, the Khatun, ruled as regent. We find Töregene Khatun taking over following the death of Ogedei, and Sorghaghtani Beki organizing the Qurultai which would see Mongke come to power. We know Genghis' wife, Börte, ruled the Mongolian homeland alongside Genghis' youngest brother Temüge. In this it appears to me that the Mongols are rather similar to the Ancient Romans, the Ottamons, or the Modern British. It would seem that women of the noble/aristocratic classes, while subordinate to men, were nonetheless deemed capable of holding power in absentia for their designated male counterparts in certain circumstances. It is plausible that one of the factors behind the ability of a group to forge a large empire was their ability to harness their aristocratic women to ensure political stability at home while the men were away. On the other hand, cultures which heavily subordinated women, refusing to let them hold power and strongly resisting any attempt to do so, were more prone to internal instability and thus unable to create or maintain large empires. We notice that as women seemed to become more subordinated in the Mongol political structures as their cultures merged with local traditions, their ability to maintain stability also appears to diminish. The role and importance of women in maintaining and continuing power therefore might be an interesting avenue of research. It would possible only if one approaches the study of the Mongols with the necessary objectivity, and detachment from the judgement and rhetoric that pervades the source material; and with the appropriate understanding of the roots of the belief systems, actions and opinions of groups towards each other in these areas.

References

Ashley, James R. (2004). The Macedonian Empire: The Era of Warfare Under Philip II and Alexander the Great, 359-323 B.C. McFarland.

Bertman, Stephen (2005). Handbook to Life in Ancient Mesopotamia. Oxford: Oxford University Press.

Browne, E.G. (1928). A Literary History of Persia. Vol. II. UK: Cambridge.

Flower, Harriet I. (2014). The Cambridge Companion to the Roman Republic. UK: Cambridge University Press.

Frankopan, Peter (2015). The Silk Roads; A New History of the World. London: Bloomsbury.

Haqqi, Syed A. H. (2010). Chingiz Khan; The Life and Legacy of an Empire Builder. New Delhi: Primus Books.

Juvayni, Atâ-Malek. Tārīkh-i Jahāngushāy. 1206.

Juzjani, Minhaj-i-Siraj. Tabakat-I-Nasiri. Translated by H. G. Raverty. 1260.

Lane, George (2004). Genghis Khan and Mongol Rule. USA: Greenwood Publishing Group.

Marshall, Robert (1993). Storm from the East: From Genghis Khan to Khubilai Khan. USA: University of California Press.

Mohammad, Habib, and Khaliq Ahmad Nizami (1970). A Comprehensive History of India Vol V; The Delhi Sultanate AD. 1206-1526. Delhi: People's Publishing House.

Morgan, David (1994). "Persian perceptions of Mongols and Europeans." In Implicit Understandings: Observing, Reporting, and Reflecting on the Encounters between Europeans and Other Peoples in the Early Modern Era, by Stuart B. Schwartz, 201-217. UK: Cambridge University Press.

----- (1986). The Mongols. Oxford: Basil Blackwell.

Rossabi, Morris (1994). All the Khan's Horses. Asian Topics in World History Columbia University. http://afe.easia.columbia.edu/ mongols/conquests/khans_horses.pdf (accessed March 25, 2016).

Sun, Wei Kwei, trans. (1957). The Secret History of the Mongol Dynasty. Utter Pradesh: Aligarh Muslim University.

Sverdrup, Carl (2010). Numbers in Mongol Warfare. In Journal of Medieval Military History Vol VIII, by John France. UK: Boydell & Brewer.

Turnbull, Stephen (2014). Genghis Khan & the Mongol Conquests 1190–1400. Osprey Publishing.

Endnotes

1. See (Marshall 1993) and (Morgan, The Mongols 1986)
2. Such as John Mason Smith, largely relying on Juzjani, for a more complete analysis see (Sverdrup 2010)
3. (Rossabi 1994, 1)
4. In general cavalry archer bows were outraged by infantry archers, and hence had to compensate with mobility and speed
5. (Rossabi 1994, 2)
6. Recorded in contemporary literature
7. (Turnbull 2014, 17)
8. (Turnbull 2014)(Morgan, The Mongols 1986)
9. (Lane 2004)
10. (Flower 2014)(Ashley 2004)
11. See for instance (Haqqi 2010)
12. (Bertman 2005)

CHAPTER - NINE

Historical Consciousness in Pre Modern India

Vandana Rana

Did historical consciousness exist in pre modern India before the arrival of British? Clearly, the Indian subcontinent had a past of some kind but various historians and other Scholars have wondered whether Indians of the pre modern were aware of the empirical character of the past or not. A thousand years ago Al-biruni complained that "unfortunately" the Hindus do not pay much attention to the historical order of things. According to him, Hindus were very careless in maintaining the chronological order of things and when they pressed for information they often took to tale telling. But there is a need to understand this concept that history was an "alien" import brought in by colonial rule, in a more renounced and Critical way.

The very idea of treating history as a scientific, rational and objective discipline is a modern construct. One should try to understand the earlier modes of into the past in its own terms in which various kinds of literary forms played a crucial role. C.A Bayly has argued in the same line when he wrote that process of Indo Persian history writing of the 18th century has a distinct "Indian Acumen". Similarly, V Narayan Rao, David Shuleman and Sanjay Subramanyam have explored the field of history writing in the 18 century, in the context of Indian subcontinent. There are other historians as well who have highlighted that there were people in pre modern India who actually thought that they were involved in the writing process. Romila Thapar, Prachi Deshpande and Kumkum Chatterjee talk about such history writing traditions in pre-colonial India. This essay will try to throw light on these ideas and will ultimately argue that a tradition of history writing and a kind of historical consciousness even among the pre modern Indians but to understand it one has to see these traditions not with the lenses which sees history as an objective and empirical discipline but by acknowledging their distinct nature and the surroundings in which they were written.

The modern concept of rational and scientific discipline can be traced back to the 19th Century Europe where it is seen as a medium to explore "past realities" on the basis of verifiable evidence, studied objectively. This concept of history narrowed the domain of history. It excluded all those modes of remembering the past from the category of history which do not fit in this definition. Thus, this classified many societies as a "historical" before the arrival of Europeans such as South Asia, Africa and Latin America where the accounts of remembering the past are not considered as historical text. These areas, hence according to the European observers had no tradition of history writing. When British Colonial rule was established in India then many British writers James Mill, Thomas Batington Macaulay etc. expressed disdain about the inability of Indians to write proper history.

But as Kumkum Chatterjee has argued that it is true that the British Colonial rule brought a new way of history writing to Indian subcontinent but then it cannot be automatically assumed that Pre modern India not have any historical consciousness. History writing in pre modern India was not a specialized practice associated with formal institutions. As Romila Thapar noted that it was a practice which was "embedded" in various kinds of narratives, thereby sometimes tendering it difficult for modern readers, accustomed to regarding history as a self-contained "exclusive" discipline to identify in a material which defied such characterization. The modern definition of history seeing it as rational positivist discipline fails to recognize the various modes of writing history in pre modern India when literary forms like "*Kavya*", use of verses instead of prose etc. were used as a means to write history. This pre modern historiography is seen by European Scholars as lacking a proper methodology and distinction between what is factual and what is fictional. In contrast to this V. Narayan Rao, David Shulman and Sanjay Subramanyam have argued that the audience of that time was able to distinguish between factual and fictional. So, it is necessary to view pre modern historiography with a different perspective.

Rao, Shuleman, and Subramanyam has shown that there are narratives of the pre modern time which are based on facts and focuses the state and inform about the credibility of the sources and also bound by secular casual explanation but such narratives come from a literary genres like poems, ballads from the itihas-purana tradition. Yet these narratives were considered by their readers or listeners as historical narratives. So, according to them the tradition history writing was present in India much before the arrival of the British.

There is no dearth of such kind of texts in pre modern India. For instance, Prachi Deshpande has discussed the distinct prediction of Bakhar writings which recorded history of a lineage or of a family of property or political dominance or of significant events, in the western part of India, in the Marathi speaking region. She has shown how Bakhar placed events in a sequence and showed why and how they happened through a literary recreation of the past. Sumit Guha has also highlighted that Bakhar emerged as a local factual narratives and he viewed their literary and historical qualities together rather than separating them.

Apart From Bakhar tradition there were also other texts which were written in pre modern time as historical texts but now they are not considered as historical documents. For example in North East India particularly in Assam Buranji, tradition became a source of writing history in pre-colonial Assam. Yasmin Saikia points out that the first evidence of Buranji came during the 17th century but she says distinct pre-colonial tradition of writing history as very different from the Indo Persian style which already existed at that time. In pre-colonial India often the historical text were written in only that language which represented the political Elite class of that time. Thus, before the Turkish invasion it was more or less Sanskrit and in the Mughal period person became dominant. Kumkum Chatterjee in her work *The Culture of History in India: Persianization and Mughal Culture in Bengal* has explored how the practice of history writing during the early modern was influenced by the prevailing Persian culture. According to her, writing in the early modern was not about repeating unchanging notions of the past rather it served as political and cultural statements derived from their immediate environment. She showed how historiographical narratives during the 17th century and 18th centuries in Bengal were primarily written in Sanskrit or Bengali but during this period they showed a remarkable shift in terms of content and idioms. The new elements were drawn from the Persian language. Another example where historical text were written in pre modern India but not as poem in the present day dominant format of pros but as poems which is highlighted by Allison Bucsh in her essay *Literary Responses to the Mughal Imperium : The Historical Poems of Keshav Das*. She has focused mainly on three works of Keshavdas *Ratanbavani, Virsimhdivacarita* and *Jahangirjascandrika*.

Thus, to acknowledge the historical writings or the tradition of history writing in pre modern India there is a need to understand history in pre modern India has been written in many genres and that writing history was not a matter of strict adherence to formal characteristics and types, a point raised by Romila Thapar. In pre modern India the choice of genre or mode for historiographical purposes frequently changed over time, as a community changed its preferred modes of literary production. In such cases, when we shift from one genre to another takes place, the earlier genre loses patronage, it also tends to lose its historicity and become more literary. Thus, history is written in the dominant literary genre of a particular community, located in space and even moment in time. If *purana* is pre-eminent literary form, history will be written as *Purana* if *Kavya* dominates, we will find history as *Kavya*. But it is important to that in such genre one would find both historical and non-historical texts. So, one should able to distinguish between the two with the help of markers, shifters, lexical choices etc.

Thus, the earlier moons of related to the past should be understood in the context of that period. In the pre modern time literary forms were generally used to write historical accounts but European observers relegated those accounts to the category of fictions and declared that Indian subcontinent lacked historical consciousness during the pre-modern time. By examining various pre modern text, historical text written in different literary genre one could get a more nuanced understanding India's rich history writing tradition which existed even before the colonial period.

References

Lukacs, John (1968). Historical Consciousness: The Remembered Past. USA: Harper and Row.

Lukacs, John (2004). Remembered Past: John Lukacs on History, Historians and Historical Knowledge. USA: ISI Books.

Section –III
Modern History

CHAPTER - TEN

The Influence of Ancient Rome on the French Revolution and its Potential for Class Analysis

TCA Achintya

The French Revolution is not a phenomenon that most historians set out to analyse lightly. The pivotal procession of events set in motion in 1789 with the Estates General, and the Tennis Court Oath, would lead not just to political changes in France, but would reverberate across the world. The Revolution overthrew the monarchy of France, established the First French Republic, experienced violent periods of political and social turmoil, and finally culminated in a dictatorship by Napoleon that rapidly carried many of its principles to Western Europe and beyond. Inspired by liberal and radical ideas, the Revolution profoundly affected the course of modern history, triggering a near-global decline of absolute monarchies and replacing them with republics. Through the Revolutionary Wars, it unleashed a wave of conflicts that would extend from the Caribbean to the Middle East. It is for this reason that many historians regard it as one of the most important events in human history.

The modern era has unfolded in the shadow of the French Revolution. Almost all subsequent revolutionary movements looked back to it as their predecessor. Its central phrases and cultural symbols, such as La Marseillaise and *Liberté, Egalité,*

Fraternité, became the clarion call for other major upheavals, including the Russian Revolution over a century later. The values and institutions of the Revolution dominate French politics to this day.

But the French Revolution itself was not an event free of symbolism and influence. Much like how it would itself be a source of inspiration, incentive and impulse for political ideologies and philosophies, revolutionary movements and national polities, its people were also inspired and motivated by inherited beliefs and notions.

One of the brightest guiding lights of European thought was the institution of Ancient Rome. Both the Roman Republic and the Roman Empire would provide inspiration in the form of symbols, of political and philosophical ideas, and as a source of legitimacy. The Imperium of Rome represented both authority and idealism, and so in various ways it would provide the necessary basis for many different types of political and philosophical movements.

The Roman inspiration for the French Revolution was not from a single source, however. While the idea and ethos of Rome's Empire and Republic certainly played a direct role in shaping the ideas of Revolutionary France and its immediate predecessors and successors, there were many indirect influences as well. Among the strongest influences on the French revolutionaries, for instance, had been the American Revolution. The founding fathers of America, in turn, had been heavily influenced by the ideals of Rome's Republic.

As Mortimer Sellers writes in the essay "The Roman Republic and the French and American Revolutions" (Flower, 2014)[1]

> A new "Senate" would meet on the "Capitol" Hill, overlooking the "Tiber" river (formerly "Goose Creek"), as in Rome, to restore "the sacred fire of liberty" to the Western world. The vocabulary of eighteenth century revolution reverberated with purposeful echoes of

republican Rome as political activists self-consciously assumed the Roman mantle. James Madison and Alexander Hamilton, the primary authors and advocates of the United States Constitution, wrote together pseudonymously as "Publius" to defend their creation, associating themselves with Publius Valerius Poplicola, founder and first consul of the Roman Republic. Camille Desmoulins attributed the French Revolution to Cicero's ideal of Roman politics, imbibed by children in the schools. At every opportunity, American and French revolutionaries proclaimed their desire to re-establish the "stupendous fabrics" of republican government that had fostered liberty at Rome.

The Roman name of "republic" evoked first and above all the memory of government without kings. Roman authors dated their republic from the expulsion of Rome's last king, Tarquinius Superbus, and mourned its fall in the principate of Augustus. As French and American politicians came increasingly into conflict with their own monarchs, they found a valuable ideology of opposition already fully formed in the Roman senatorial attitude towards Caesar and his successors. The guiding principle of this republican tradition, as remembered (for example) by Thomas Paine, was government for the "res-publica, the public affairs, or the public good," perceived as naturally antithetical to monarchy and to any other form of arbitrary rule. Paine and other eighteenth century republicans viewed the individual and collective well-being of citizens as the only legitimate purpose of government. Their rallying cry of "liberty" signified subjection to laws made for the common good, and to nothing and to no one else. Statesmen traced this principle to the frequently cited passage in Livy that attributes the liberty of Rome to Lucius Junius Brutus and to his introduction of elected magistrates into Roman politics, constrained by the rule of law.

The influence of the institution of Rome did not merely exist with the Republicans, pushing an anti-monarchic agenda. Thinkers like Montesquieu and Rousseau would also be strongly influenced by the notions inherent in the ideas presented by Rome's example. While the Republicanists would look to Rome's Republic for ideological inspiration, others would look to the Principate under the likes of Augustus Caesar and Claudius to find for themselves the necessary synthesis between monarchy and parliamentary representation. Where the Republican looked at the "inherent" liberality of the Roman Republic's mode of governance, the Monarchist would point to its demise, reiterating the arguments of Tacitus and Galba, who argued that the republic was unsustainable in practice for large states (Tactius), was too fragile, and needed the state needed the stability of the Imperium and a monarch (Tacitus).

The emblems associated with "Roman Authority" would be automatic symbols of authority and legitimacy as well. Thus in the course of the French Revolution, the *fasces* (Censer & Hunt, 2001), a sign of authority and legitimacy from the Roman Era, would be used in conjunction with symbols of liberty from the era, such as the Freedman's cap (Harden, February 1995), and symbols of heroism, such as a crown wreathed in laurel (Censer & Hunt, 2001).

As many authors have pointed out, the influence of these concepts was quite pervasive. And the idea of the deep and pervasive nature of the influence of Rome lies not just with historians of the modern period. Hobbes would, for instance, note this influence in Leviathan, over a century before the American and French Revolutions, writing: "Cicero, and other writers [who] have grounded their Civil doctrine, on the opinions of the Romans, who were taught to hate Monarchy..." (Wright, 2006)

It is important to keep in mind that this influence need not necessarily have been "historically accurate". The thinkers and academics of the era would often "construct" the interpretation of what constituted a Roman influence. The most famous example could perhaps be the Roman Salute. The imagery of the salute doesn't come from strong historical sources. The Salute is strongly accepted as being a "Roman Practice" and as such, the idea of the salute and liberty and loyalty, became inextricably linked. Yet, when the 576 members of the Third Estate performed it at the Tennis Court Oath, or when Jacques-Louis David depicted it in his famous 1792 painting,[2] the inspiration did not come from an actual historical source; rather, it came from the constructed imagination of the salute by the same painter from his earlier 1784 painting, The Oath of the Horatii.[3] Some of the "ideals" and symbols of the Roman era were thus not reconstructions, rather imaginations of phenomenon.

Thus, the influence symbolism of Ancient Rome was neither accidental nor wholly sub-conscious. The Roman ideal, whether indirectly imported from America, or directly from the original city herself, was often portrayed consciously. The various thinkers of the era were aware of the links they were drawing to Rome, indeed they actively sought to locate, even create these links. As the writings of American revolutionary thinkers (Flower, 2014) show clearly, and the writings of French revolutionaries slightly less so, the identification of the political leaders at the time with politicians and heroes of the Roman Republic and Empire was deliberate and considered.

It is this intersection of symbol and inspiration that drives my argument regarding the nature of class when discussing the French Revolution. The issue of class in the French Revolution is something many historians have pondered over, and widely accepted its identification as a form of class struggle. While the most fervent advocates of this consensus are the Marxist or Classic thinkers, they are hardly alone. The primary development of the class struggle theory, of seeing the Revolution as essentially a bourgeois revolution, was predominantly the work of Georges Lefebvre[4] and Albert Soboul[5]. Lefebvre would, for instance, argue that the French Revolution began as an aristocratic revolution by the Assembly of Notables and the Paris Parliament of 1788, with the "popular revolution" being symbolized by the actions of the Third Estate and the fall of the Bastille.

The interpretation of seeing the revolution as a struggle between classes, however, is not in itself of Marxist origins. Well before Lefebvre, authors such as Francois Guizot and Alexis De Tocqueville (Furet, 1989) had elucidated the idea of seeing the French Revolution in terms of a contest between the aristocratic class and the popular class (The Third Estate) well before the popularization of Marx's historical approach. Other authors like Furet, while refuting the Marxist interpretation,[6] do tend to accept the notion of seeing a class conflict, or at least a perception of a class conflict, among its participants, for the Revolution.

It is my opinion that this notion of class could perhaps be linked to the influence of Rome as well. Even during the Republican era, Rome was a highly hierarchical society. The primary divide in Ancient Roman Society was on the basis of ancestry (Flower, 2014). The population of Roman citizens was divided into Patricians and Plebeians (Garnsey & Saller, 1987)[7]. The Patricians, in institutional form known as the Patriciate, were the "fathers" of Roman society; the original aristocrats among the Roman citizenry, and fixed in their composition. Only by adoption into a patrician family could a Roman citizen be counted as a patrician, and families themselves (the base political unit in the Roman State) could not change their status from Plebeian to Patrician. The primary legislative and governing body of the Roman State, the Senate, was thus formed predominantly by Senators of the Patriciate. Following the legendary Conflict of Orders however, and the gradual dwindling of the original Patriciate, more and more Plebeian families became senatorial. Some of the most famous Romans known to us, such as Cicero, Cato, or Pompey Magnus were Plebeians.

This brings us to the second form of social hierarchy in the system, which overlapped with ancestry. This was the census rank (*ordo*), based on the wealth and property of individuals and families. The property-based classes were thus divided into successive ranks. The highest property order was that of the Senate, with individuals requiring vast amounts of property to qualify. A member of the Senatorial class could thus stand for various political offices (except for a few lower order magistracies, such as the Tribunate of the Plebs, Military Tribune, etc). Below the *senatores* was the *ordo equester* or the Equites. Known colloquially as "Knights", the second order formed the commerce and high business class of Rome. Almost equal in terms of wealth to the census ranks of the Senators, the Equites were the elite of the Roman "Middle Class", and were often self-described as the leaders of the Plebeian classes. In most forms of Roman voting systems, be it according to Tribal classifications or according to Centuries, their class voted ahead of the lower classes, and dominated political discourse and functions. Below the Equites were three classes, each of a slightly lower property threshold than the last. At the bottom of the property ladder were the Proletarii, the working classes[8]. Finally at the bottom was the property-less Roman citizenry, the "Head Count" (*Capite Censi*) who existed as a labor class, dependent on the subsidized and free grain dole of the state, and post the era of Gaius Marius provided the bulk of Rome's military soldier class. Though they could vote, their centuries were disproportionately large, thus reducing the "value" of their individual votes to nothingness.

It is this hierarchy that we can look at for its importance in analysing the French Revolution. Identifying the First Estate and the Aristocrats with the Patriciate is hardly a new proposition. Guizot had proposed this identification as far back as the first half of the 19th century (Furet, 1989, pp. 134-136). However, this identification should carry with it a corollary; which is to see the Third Estate as being akin to the Plebeian orders. This can be particularly useful both in the context of analysing arguments such as those of Tocqueville, who saw in the Revolution the emergence of a "new aristocracy" within the Third Estate, part of a process he called the "democratization" of the society. While historians such as Furet have pointed out lacunae in the argumentation, there is a fundamental parallel that can perhaps be retained. Holding the aristocracy similar to the Patriciate-Senatorial class of Republican Rome does to a large extent hold true, because much like the aristocracy of Pre-Revolutionary France, wealthy members of the "lower orders" had in fact managed to gain ascendancy into this class. These new aristocrats were often some of the staunchest defenders of aristocratic liberties, arguing not very differently from the *Optimate*[9] politicians of the Late Republic like Cato or Cicero, despite their having risen from a lower Plebeian order[10].

The voicing of this comparison of the Aristocrats to the Patricians in the few short decades post the French Revolution, and the high involvement of Roman ideals, conscious and subconscious, in political and philosophical dialogue of the Pre- and Post-Revolutionary era, leads me to conclude that a similar notion of class according to Roman ideals of hierarchy and societal ordering may well have been present among the leaders of the Third Estate and the later Revolutionary leaders of the National Assembly, even the Directorate and later the first Consulate. The notion of the "new aristocracy" as elucidated by Tocqueville holds value not for the emergence of a discrete and unified property-owning class within the Third Estate (something historians such as Furet have disputed rather effectively) but rather the emergence of an intellectual elite, whose members who saw themselves as the leaders of the lower orders, the rest of the Third Estate, the analogues of the lower orders, the Proletarii and the Head Count, as it were.

It should be noted that viewing the organization of classes within Revolutionary French Society need not be as a contradiction or a refutation to other conceptualizations of class within that society. The Marxist interpretation for instance could also hold true, since the sub-division of the classes doesn't contradict the notion of a Bourgeois class. The point about construction of symbolism needs to be kept in mind here. Roman society was not being literally recreated by the thinkers of Revolutionary Europe. Rather it was being imaginatively reconstructed. This was a subjective exercise, not an objective one, involving significant input of interpretation, and often ideological creation. Thus, the symbolism of the Roman class structure could well be looked at, but like the Roman Salute, it need not actually match the specifics of the property classification system of Ancient Rome. When the Revolutionary leaders spoke of active and passive citizens, or when a sovereignty of the People was spoken about, the ideology can be linked to that of the *Populesque Romanus*[11] without necessarily locating historical accuracy and conformity to detail in the ideology.

Lastly, the ideological role of the Monarchy must also be kept in mind. It is easy to fall into the trap of ignoring the symbolism of the Monarchy by getting caught up in the Revolutionary rhetoric that would occur during and in the aftermath of the trial and execution of Louis XVI and his wife. However, as pointed out above, the role of the Monarch within a republican and even a Roman conceptualization of society was not a contradiction. Division of societal classes and interpreting the revolution as a Plebeian-Patrician struggle or indeed attempting to investigate whether such notions were present in the actors of the Revolution, need not run contrary to the presence of the King. Rome, in the form of the Principate, and in the body of authors such as Tacitus or Livy, provided symbolism and inspiration as well.

I would conclude by suggesting an interesting thought experiment - to view the Revolution of France as being a process which would run in a stream opposite to the course Rome took. Where in Rome, the struggle of the classes started from the Plebeians gaining power, to the Upper classes fighting back,[12] and the resultant conflict eventually resulting in stability being achieved under a Monarch who moderated the power of the Patricians, France would see the Absolute Monarchy face a revolt from its Aristocrats, which would devolve into a struggle between the Patricians and the Plebs. One can locate significant ideological similarities and justifications across the two processes, and given the high degree of awareness and drive for identification with Rome among contemporary thinkers of that era, it might be valid to assume that there was in fact a deliberate and conscious emulation of Roman ideals - not just visible symbolism, but in the ideological struggle itself. Leaders like Robespierre may well have genuinely viewed themselves akin to the *Equites,* the leaders of the Plebeians against the Aristocratic Patricians.

Reference

Censer, J., & Hunt, L. (2001). Liberty, Equality, and Fraternity: Exploring the French Revolution. Retrieved from http://chnm.gmu.edu/revolution/chap12j.html

Censer, J., & Hunt, L. (2001). Liberty, Equality, Fraternity: Exploring the French Revolution. Retrieved from http://chnm.gmu.edu/revolution/chap12i.html

David, J.-L. (1784). The Oath of the Horatii. Louvre Paris. Retrieved 05 22, 2017, from https://upload.wikimedia.org/wikipedia/commons/3/35/Jacques-Louis_David%2C_Le_Serment_des_Horaces.jpg

David, J.-L. (1791). Le Serment du Jeu de paume. Musée national du Château de Versailles. Retrieved 05 22, 2017, from https://upload.wikimedia.org/wikipedia/commons/6/6d/Le_Serment_du_Jeu_de_paume.jpg

Flower, H. I. (2014). The Cambridge Companion to the Roman Republic. Cambridge University Press.

Furet, F. (1989). Interpreting the French Revolution. (E. Forster, Trans.) Cambridge University Press.

Garnsey, P., & Saller, R. (1987). The Roman Empire: Economy, Society and Culture. Berkeley.

Harden, J. (February 1995). Libtery Caps and Libtery Trees. Past & Present No. 146, 66-102.

Tacitus. (n.d.). Annalium Libri.

Tactius. (n.d.). Historiarum libri.

Wright, G. (2006). Religion, Politics and Thomas Hobbes. In G. Wright. Springer.

Endnotes

1   Section 5 of The Cambridge Companion to the Roman Republic has influenced and is the source of much of the first few paragraphs of the article when discussing the general influence of Roman on Modern Thought.

2   (David, Le Serment du Jeu de paume, 1791)

3   (David, The Oath of the Horatii, 1784)

4   *Les paysans du Nord* published 1924 and *The Great Fear of 1789*, published 1932, translated to English 1973

5   *The Sans-Culottes* published 1968

6   In *La Révolution Française* in 1965-66

7   Information presented in the following paragraphs about Roman society has been primarily researched from the Cambridge Companion to the Roman Republic as well as the Roman Empire: Economy, Society and Culture. However, my first introduction to the classes of Rome, and their overall similarity to the issue of revolutionary class struggle is inspired by the works of Colleen McCullough, author of the Masters of Rome series, a collection of Historical Fiction novels, acclaimed for their high degree of historical accuracy

8   And the root for the Marxist Proletariat Class, a further example of the depth of Roman Influence in philosophical thinking and constructs

9   Also known as the *boni* or "the Good Men", famously the political opponents of Popularist politicians like Gaius Marius, Saturnius and Julius Caesar

10 Cicero for instance was famously derided as a "Homo Novus" or a New Man, ie one with non-distinguished ancestry outside of Rome, while Cato was famously descended from the Slave-Wife of the famous Cato the Censor

11 People of Rome, part of the SPQR – Senatus Populesque Romanus – The Senate and People of Rome

12 Under Sulla for instance

CHAPTER - ELEVEN

Development of Indian Archaeology till the Close of the 19th Century

Srotoswini Borah

The Historical study of ancient India cannot be understood by discussing the textual sources alone. The sources which are regarded as important are not historical sources and whatever historical information can be gathered from or has been gathered from these texts are not free from biases. There always arise the questions regarding the chronology, geographical applicability and even the context. There is paucity in historical works which cannot be regarded as the ultimate sources for the reconstruction of Indian archaeology.

Archaeology can massively expand the nature of the sources in the context of ancient India. The research in archaeological field always leads to the unobserved aspects of the historical landscape. If we talk about ancient India, the basic quantity and the accuracy of textual documentation are comparatively limited. So, in this condition, the archaeological research always becomes very significant to extract the exact truth of the ancient Indian past to a greater extent.

The task of determining the chronology of an artifact is can be regarded as only a half part of the work of an archaeologist. Another half part is mainly consisted of the task of reconstructing the ancient culture from which the artifact comes. This process is commonly known as the contextual analysis. The lowest or most initial level of contextual analysis consists of analyzing the systems of subsistence and technology or to analyze the ways in which ancient people adapted to their environment. The next level is concerned with the reconstruction of the social structure and the settlement patterns of these people. Finally, an archaeologist tries to reconstruct the essence of a culture or the guiding beliefs.

Each of these levels requires different analytical methods. Archaeologists may start reconstructing an ancient subsistence system by determining what the people ate. They may do this through coprology, the examination of fossilized feces, or by analyzing human bones for the presence of certain forms of carbon and nitrogen. The study of the plant remains found in a dig can also provide clues to a people's diet. By studying ancient tools—such as arrow tips, butcher knives, and grinding stones—archaeologists can find out how people obtained and prepared their foods. Archaeologists may also be able to determine how ancient people made and used their tools. Studying the work of a modern flint knapper, for instance, may show an archaeologist how ancient people made flint tools. (In archaeology, this type of reasoning or interpretation is called ethnographic analogy.)

When archaeologists attempt to reconstruct ancient social structures, they often use data gathered by ethnographers, social anthropologists, and historians. The excavated materials themselves may also provide hints of ancient social organization. Specialized artifacts that are found concentrated in certain areas may indicate that the ancient culture had full-time craft specialists, and different types of burial arrangements may indicate that social classes existed.

Reconstructing the highest level of a culture, including its values, ethos, or religion, is the most difficult type of contextual analysis. Such items as statues or paintings of figures that appear to be supernatural, buildings that may have been temples, and evidence of religious ceremonies can all be used to help reconstruct ancient systems of beliefs.

When we look at the archaeological development in India, we can notice three groups of people who came to India during the 16th century. These groups comprised of the Portuguese people of Goa, the other European sailors and the other Western travellers. Mainly, two types of monuments attracted the eyes of the Europeans which were comprised of the West Indian rock cut caves mainly the Elephanta caves of the West and the other monuments consisted of the Konark and the Jagannatha temples of Orissa in the East. Italian sailor Pietro della Valle visited India during the phase between 1623–1625 and drew the ground plans of South Indian temples. So, these can be regarded as the early approaches. But, it is important to note that till that time there was no significant development in the field of Indian archaeology. The European migration, however, in reality opened the doors to the development of Indian archaeology and helped in reconstructing the ancient Indian past.

The actual beginning of Indian archaeology can be traced back to the middle part of the 18th century. During this time, some scholars like Anquetil du Parron and Danish engineer Carsten Niebuhr altogether put forward the need for a systematic and scholarly study of Indian antiquities. Many famous historical sites were begun to be studied. By the middle of the 18th century there emerged an interest among various European scholars to identify the major ancient Indian cities like Pataliputra on the ground. However, It is important to note that the correct identification of Pataliputra with the modern day Patna had to wait till 1788 when a book of an English geographer known as '*Memoir of a Map of Hindustan*' came into being. The book was mainly concerned with the work of James Rennell on the Indian historical geography during the period of 1786 till 1788.

It is important to mention here that in the 2nd half of the 18th century there began a considerable philosophical interest in the antiquity of India in Europe, particularly among the French philosophers. But, till that time there was no prominent Indian who had any interest in the study of Indian antiquities. So, the development of Indian archaeology was only centered on the works of the Europeans.

The establishment of the Asiatic Society in Calcutta on 15th January 1784 brought a new dimension to the archaeological development in India. After the establishment of this society, a hunger became prominent among the Europeans to know about the country systematically they were about to rule. The establishment did not initiate archaeological research in India, but it acted as a motivation in the study of Indian antiquities by the Europeans in India. Archaeological discoveries were scanty till the 1830's. But there came into publication of Francis Buchanan's three volume report on Mysore in 1807, survey on Bengal Presidency in 1816 and a three-volume summary again of the Bengal Presidency was published in 1838. These were actually statistical surveys but contain a fair proportion of archaeological information. On the other side, Colin Mackenzie began a study of the antiquities in South India through his collection of manuscripts and inscriptions.

Another legendary character in the initiation of field research in India was James Prinsep. He became the Secretary of the Asiatic Society by the early 1830's. His work became significant after he succeeded in the decipherment of the two most important historical scripts of India i.e. *Brahmi* and *Kharoshthi*. With the decipherment of the two ancient scripts, rapid development was made in the fields of epigraphical and numismatic studies. This led to the proper understanding of the chronological order of the historical sites in India. There also began some attempts to understand Buddhist legends on the basis of the two Sri Lankan chronicles i.e. the *Dipavamsa* and the *Mahavamsa*. An important result of this was the discovery of the name Asoka in these Buddhist chronicles.

Another eminent personality in the history of Indian archaeology is Alexander Cunningham who came to India at an early age of 18 and rose to the rank of Major-General from the initial post of a military engineer. He was deeply inspired by the work of Prinsep and decided to go to the far of places of India and explore the ancient Indian sites by his own. Cunningham's work was mainly inspired by the travelogue of Fa-Hien who was a Chinese pilgrim to India. Cunningham used the itinerary of Fa-Hien to determine the bearing of Sankisa in relation to Mathura. He travelled extensively and wrote detailed descriptions of the areas he visited and their distances and directions from each other. The accounts of the two Chinese pilgrims i.e. Fa-Hien and Xuanzang (Hiuen-Tsang) were translated into French and published in the 1830's. Cunningham realized the great significance of these accounts in fixing the locations of major archaeological sites.

In 1848, he offered a scheme of archaeological investigations to the Government of India it took a long time for this scheme to be implemented, but ultimately the Archaeological Survey of India came into existence in 1861 with Alexander Cunningham as its head. The Government of India discontinued the work of the Survey during the period of 1866 to 1870, but Cunningham continued his work till 1885. The results of his and his assistants' works were incorporated in a series of volumes which still regarded as essential reading for the study of Indian archaeology. Cunningham had the specific target of reconstructing the ancient historical geography of India by settling it with actual sites and monuments. The explorations of Alexander Cunningham were mainly relied on immense hardship with high enduring capacity because the explorations were mainly done on horseback, elephants, camel and even on foot which were very much problematic.

One interesting aspect of the explorations of Cunningham is that he used to by whole fields of grain from their owners when he came to know that the places were known to have yielded antiquities previously. Many people of indigenous origin of India helped in the explorations of Cunningham. Out of them mention may be made of Raja Siva Prasad who helped him in finding the remains of the Gupta dynasty in India. Many helped him in the collection of coins and location of sites and even for their inspections. However, it is important to note that the explorations of Cunningham at a later time developed into nothing but merely object-hunting expeditions because it can be seen that he collected a large number of ancient inscriptions and sculptures.

It is however important to note that the participation of the Indians in Indian Archaeological studies show the consciousness of the English-educated Indian elite effected by the sense of the ancient Indian past in different parts of the country. From the very beginning of the early 16th century to the closing years of the 19th century, the cautious footsteps of Indian archaeology can easily be traced. At the dawn of the 20th century there was a definite archaeological shape of ancient Indian past. However, this achievement cannot cover up some important aspects to be analyzed. Firstly, the role of the Government in this field of development of archaeology was limited. The Archaeological Survey of India which was founded in 1861 suffered a lot of interruptions before the end of the 19th century. Secondly, the important task of preserving the ancient Indian monuments was to a greater extent regarded as a complete failure. The special post of the Curator of ancient monuments was created in 1880 and lasted for three years after which the responsibility of conservation passed on to the provincial governments and ultimately to the Public Works Departments. Thirdly, there was no systematic process of excavation of the ancient historic settlements. The excavations in reality were taken place in a haphazard way. In fact, in the closing years of 19th century the Government had no bigger plans for the development of Indian archaeology except a province-wise listing of the major monuments and sites.

The archaeological development was thus mainly contributed by the works of the European powers. The European trading groups who came to India with the motive of expansion of trade finally contributed towards the exploration of the various archaeological sites of ancient India. The identification of the ancient Indian sites with the present day places however gave a significant essence to the forgotten history of ancient India. The scientific expeditions and explorations can be regarded as the most important development of Indian archaeology. Though these explorations led to the growing hunger of the Europeans for the ancient Indian antiquities, at the same time these explorations opened up the study of archaeology in India. The archaeological development by the Europeans however led to the destruction of many ancient Indian sites due to the haphazard way of exploration. The identification of ancient Indian cities also resulted in the looting of many ancient Indian antiquities. But above all, it is important to mention here that the development of Indian archaeology can be regarded as a gift of the adventurous Europeans. This ultimately opened a new dimension in the study of ancient Indian antiquities for the construction of the nation's past. Chronology became crucial for the proper development of archaeology and history for which the Europeans gave much importance. The 19th century's archaeology of India talks about the development of archaeological practice in India. Though it is important to know the context in which the various archaeological writings were constructed by the Europeans. In reality, Indian archaeology was influenced by the social and political factors in the interpretation of archaeological data and the preservation of cultural heritage. Thus, the development of Indian archaeology ultimately led to the discovery of the Indus Valley civilization by the Europeans which can be regarded as a significant step towards the proper development of ancient Indian culture and heritage.

References

Maiti, P. (1964). Studies in Ancient India. Kolkata: Shreedhar Prakashani.

Sharma, R.S. (2005). India's Ancient Past. Oxford: Oxford University Press.

Singh, Upinder (2009). A History of Ancient and Early Medieval India. New Delhi: Pearson Education India.

Jain, V.K. (2006). Prehistory and Protohistory of India. New Delhi: D.K. Printworld.

CHAPTER - TWELVE

Archaeology and Museums: Rethinking Sense of Identity in India

Rajeev Kumar

Introduction

Indian history was obscure, till the 18th century, with certain doubts and discrepancies regarding the data, dates and developments through ages. Chronology for a certain epoch in the Indian past could hardly be fixed with conviction. Whatever record was there was solely based upon the textual tradition which could not go beyond the 2nd millennium BC. The turnaround, which made this question of uncertainty answerable to an extent, came with the discovery of the methodology of archaeology in India. Though this was the unintended result of the British subjugation, it helped in bringing accuracy of description and documentation of the material remains and their visual and textual record for deriving objective knowledge about the past.

Early interest in natural history initiated the interest in museums. From their beginnings, archaeological museums have reflected a complex and dynamic balance between the demands of developing, documenting, and preserving objects on the one hand and sharing knowledge, access, and control on the other[1]. In India they were, however, results of private collections. In the 20th century (post-independence) the archaeological museums became significant and the government museums started collecting antiquities and promoting museums as tool of education. In rejecting the Indian identity built with the colonial Indological framework of race, language and culture, archaeological knowledge gained from museums played very crucial role. They helped in dismantling the old colonial identity of India and putting in its place a sense of identity shared by all categories of Indians. This was made possible by providing time-bound and area-bound perspective of the history of the Indians which museums are practically adept at doing.

Archaeology in India

The past of a nation is glorified through the presence of available records, written and material, reflecting the eminence of the past. A strong base right from the antiquity to pre-modern times and even later, is created through chronological developments that are maintained in the records trying to portray the achievements the nation has acquired over time. The written records, though of immense value, are susceptible to subjectivity. Thus, the material remains fill in the gap to know the society in entirety and present a real and objective picture of the past, thereby substantiating the true picture of the events that took place in the past. This makes going beyond the texts a prerequisite to knowing the past. The material remains that we get through excavations fall in the domain of archaeology.

The term 'archaeology' was introduced in India during the latter half of the 19th century, coinciding with the British Raj, and it related to the material remains of the past, artefacts, sites and monuments. At the same time, the process of legitimization of the British rule rested as much on interpretation of India's past as of its present. Since then, archaeology has made exemplary strides in pre and proto Indian history, thereby assessing the cultural anthropology of the past through coins, inscriptions, monuments, etc.

When archaeology emerged as a discipline in colonial India, it was sponsored by the state and was restricted only to the historical period. The East India Company sponsored the textual study of *Dharmashastra*, a move inspired by the colonial attitude towards the objective study of the writings on Indian history, art and archaeology[2]. The Asiatic Society of Bengal best represented the spirit of antiquarian scholarship in India. Established in 1784 by William Jones, the society worked as a meeting place for European minds, harnessing their intellectual energy and potential. The trend continued into the 19th century where the investigation of India's past was again to be dominated by the European scholars. But soon after 1830, there was an increasing tendency to report and speculate on individual sites which brought into picture the 'natives' and soon they began to exert some role in deciphering the Indian past, though still limited. As a result, during James Prinsep's time, the Asiatic Society looked more towards epigraphic, numismatic and overall archaeological investigation.

Archaeological Survey of India

As the British crown began to directly administer its Indian empire, an idea increasingly gaining ground was that the public works, education, and law ought to be part of Great Britain's 'civilizing mission'. Consequently, during the 1860s and 70s, the Government became pro-active in promoting the illustration and conservation of historical monuments. To this end, the Archaeological Survey of India (ASI) was set up in 1871 to construct India's past through archaeological research.

Henry Cole was instrumental in organizing the London Exhibition (1851) showcasing the richness of Indian crafts and designs[3]. He had surveyed a lot of temples and later became the first Curator of ancient monuments of India in 1881. His contribution to the development of archaeology in India and the role of Indians in it was immense which can be gauged from his vision that the focus should more be on the maintenance rather than restoration[4]. He recognized the importance of harnessing local interest for better conservation work and revival of Indian crafts, increasingly corrupted by European influence. Thus, he was the first who raised his voice against the damage done to the historical monuments in India by the British.

In the long run, archaeological research and the conservation of historical monuments ceased to be the monopoly of the British government of India and the European scholars[5]. Many personalities outside the ASI provided dimensions to archaeology in India and some princely states, in the same vein, started collaborating with the British. Restoration at Sanchi, as for example, began in 1881 under the direction of Austin Mears and the expenses for restoration work were shared by the imperial government and Shah Jahan Begum of Bhopal[6]. Further, the 1880s saw pressures on the Archaeological Department to increase Indian participation in the archaeological expertise. Lord Ripon, in fact, had to bear the brunt of the European community in India when he was seen as having gone too far in this direction by promoting the Ilbert Bill. Consequently, Fergusson tried to demolish Babu Rajendralala Mitra's scholarly reputation by considering his architectural writings as ridiculous to show how ill-conceived the Ilbert Bill was in allowing the Indians to sit in judgement over Europeans.

The ASI under Sir John Marshall, in 1906, divided its operation into a series of reconstituted geographical areas. It also started increasing the intake of Indian scholars into its main foray. One major change in the 20th century archaeological approach was a shift from the historical period to an interest in pre- and proto-historic archaeology. Arabic, Persian and Sanskrit epigraphy were promoted and Indian scholars contributed immensely towards the same. Marshall introduced horizontal excavation, a major departure from Cunningham. Another major development was the copying and translation of inscriptions by the ASI.

In the post-Independence period, emphasis was largely laid on the study of economy which was believed to be having a bearing on the overall social structure. Archaeology, thus, became a means to understand the socio-economic history. Further in the 1980s, history and archaeology began to look more at the study of communities (peripheral or non-elite) like the craft community and the hunting community, a major departure from the colonial framework where the marginalized sections did not have any place.

Thus, from 1784 onwards till independence, the study of archaeology in India was very much in the hands of European scholars. Indian history and the various facets related to it were interpreted and presented to meet their own requirements. Indian archaeology was, thus, superimposed by the British rather than being an organic development. However, many prominent figures in Indian archaeology like R.D. Banerjee owed the rebirth of the lost entity of the Indian history to the colonial rule; the sense of identity was never inclined in favour of the Indians as the British were doing services for meeting the ends they desired.

Museums in India

Museums are complex institutions of integration of cultures where tangible and intangible traditions exhibit the man and nature relationship[7]. The material remains of the archaeological practice are preserved for times to come. Museums, thus, become part of archaeological practice. The initial interest in museums arose from the interest in natural history which was non-imperial in nature.

Museums in India have enlightened the people on different communities, their lifestyles, societies and regions extending over different time-periods in Indian history. The regional diversity and the interactions are also taken account of. In Indian context, museums have also undergone gradual catharsis. The collection of antiquities and artefacts in India had varied trajectories. The museums, in fact, resulted from the private collections. The museum movement in India started towards the close of the 18th century. Initially the scholars attached with the learned societies like the Asiatic Society of Bengal, the Madras literary Society, British administrative officials, military personnel, and native rulers[8].

Colonial Enterprise and the Archaeological Museum

With the colonial subjugation of India, Indian past was superimposed in a way to securing and legitimizing the then present rule of the colonizers. The colonial administrators and military officers collected the objects of past for profits or making gifts. In 1784, William Jones first came up with the idea of a museum for the Asian studies and in 1814 a museum of the Asiatic Society was set up. It was a society museum rather than a state museum with sections on ethnology, geology and zoology. The collection of the Society Museum was later, however, shifted to the Indian Museum in Calcutta.

Whatever was collected from the archaeological sites was placed in site museums of the specific sites. The first of this kind was set up at Mathura in 1874 by F.S. Growse. In the 20th century, the archaeological museums became more significant and special funds were created for purchase of articles and the post of a superintendent was created. The government museums became active in collection of antiquities and setting up of museums for those collections.

National Museum

In the early fervor of Independence, the formulation of a national culture was undoubtedly powered by a desire to recover India's indigenous traditions, untainted by 'external' influences of the European or the Islamic world[9]. The Markham-Hargreaves Report of 1936[10] stressed on the need for a centralized museum and in continuation of it, Mortimer Wheeler brought up a scheme for a central museum of art, archaeology and anthropology. It was meant to have the public face of the ASI. Soon after the Indian independence, an exhibition of Indian art and archaeology was held in London showcasing Indian sculptures. The exhibition proved to be a failure and was indirectly responsible for the coming up of the National Museum at Delhi. When the exhibition and the objects loaned from India came back, they were set up in an exhibition of 'Masterpieces of Indian Art' in the Durbar Hall of the Rashtrapati Bhawan[11]. The long legacy of Indian art visualized there was seen as a valuable mirror to the national self.

Finally, the National Museum of India came up on August 15, 1949. Dr Grace Morley was the first director of the National Museum and she promoted it as a tool of education. She further wanted to promote non-Indian art because having only Indian collections, according to her, made the Indian art history a study in iconography rather than a comparative study in art history. She, therefore, introduced the pre-Columbian art as the first non-Indian gallery in the National Museum. The National Museum, till India's independence, was thus controlled by the British and served their purposes.

Archaeology and Museums: Sense of Identity

While looking closely at the museums and the archaeological practices followed by them, one often comes across the pertinent question of identity. Do the museums in India, through display of past, answer the questions of identity? If yes, what sort of identity is being promoted by the museums? Do the museums promote a sense of identity at various levels of society, viz. national, regional, tribal, local and individual? Museums in India, through the art and archaeology practices, certainly promote such identities. Ever since independence, history at the museums have been dealt with some kind of objectivity where colonial exercises and mindset have been sidelined, though with mixed success.

The way a nation views its past and the significance it attaches to its heritage resembles the self-respect and identity of that nation. The Indians no longer accept the Indian identity built with the colonial Indological framework of race, language and culture (Aryan – Non-Aryan Dichotomy) as this notion keeps a vast segment of Indian population away from a sense of positive participation in the country's past. The question of identity has, thus, emerged as a major phenomenon in recent Indian reconstruction of the past. According to D.K. Chakrabarti, the notion of India built by about two centuries of Indological research was unsuitable for providing a common historical platform to all Indians[12] and thus arose the need to dismantle the old colonial Indological identity of India and put in its place a sense of identity which could be shared by all categories of Indians. He further opines that the knowledge on which this new sense of identity should be based can only be archaeological knowledge as it can provide time-bound and area-bound perspectives of the history of the Indian people.

The museums do serve the purpose of creating a sense of identity and belongingness. The Harappan gallery and other such galleries at the National Museum in New Delhi and other such museums all across India are ample proof of the process of rethinking that the historians and the archaeologists have been undergoing on the part of having a sense of identity propagated by and for indigenization.

The 'Harappan Gallery'

The most prominent change in the concept of museums in India came through thematic presentation in the galleries. The 'Harappan Gallery' at the National Museum in Delhi is an example of proven identity at various stages. It contains large numbers of artifacts from the sites of Harappan civilization. The collection includes pottery, seals, tablets, weights and measures, jewellery, terracotta figurines, toys, etc. which are all indicative of a sense of identity at various levels of society. The gallery, based on archaeological data, provides much more than any textual knowledge. It provides knowledge about different communities, their lifestyles, societies and regions, rather than simply focusing on the elite knowledge which formed the base of the colonial studies. It has taken into account the regional diversity and the inter-cultural interactions in the subcontinent from the Early Harappan Phase. The recent discovery of gold jewellery in association with other materials of Harappa genre from Mandi in Muzaffarnagar district of Uttar Pradesh shows the regional spread and extent of the Harappan material and the possible contact between different communities of the two regions. It exemplifies the fact that the display of these artefacts in the museums does convey the message of intercultural connections between different regions which could be seen in other spheres of life as well.

Material evidences from different Harappan sites attest to the fact that craft, trade and agriculture and the communities associated with them interacted with each other at local and other levels. It can also be substantiated by the fact that Harappan tools of mason, weaver, fishermen and town planner were reported from most of the mature Harappan sites. They also represent the linkages of material culture across regions. The bronze images of c. 2000 BCE from Harappa and the four bronzes of Harappan age (one chariot and three big animal figures) from Daimabad (Maharashtra), all kept in the National Museum at New Delhi, were solid cast by the lost-wax method which was the typical bronze casting technique of the Harappans. Thus, the artifacts in the museums, i.e. pottery, seals, tablets, terracotta figurines, coins, toys, etc. all help in promoting a sense of identity and interconnectedness at various levels of society.

Similarly, there are many 'tribal' groups in India and the continuous process of their absorption in the fold of Hindu caste society did not leave those indigenous groups out of the mainstream as has been intentionally portrayed by the colonial authors. They were never cut off from the social and economic forces operating around them in which they had certain functions to perform. The specificities (in duty), i.e. the functional positions appeared to reflect the hierarchy of the caste system. However, the diversity of functions has been succinctly brought forth through the drawing of conjectural pictures of the Lothal dockyard. The depiction of various occupations of Indians, around 2600-2000 BC, have been drawn through persons performing various functions in a community. This is a clear indication of the involvement of various persons in a community in various skilled craftsmanship as well as works at community level like community water-release system. They were locally active and produced things for their own consumption. But at the same time their art clearly suggests their contacts with other parts of the world. The use of lapis lazuli for making necklaces is a fine example of their overseas networks.

Every area has its traditional historical linkages and interacts within the orbit thus created. In its turn, an individual interacts with other orbits, leading to an image of many historically interacting orbits. There are innumerable examples of this kind of development from different areas of the subcontinent. In fact, the interaction between different sections within the country – the interdependence for raw materials – is deeply rooted in the Harappan civilization and well depicted in the gallery of the National Museum. Chakrabarti, however, argues that the sense of identity, post-independence, has been formed on the basis of caste, religion and region rather than one single national identity[13]. He argues that the nationalists have not criticized the Aryan notion to its core which is the most important reason why such notions still exist and we are unable to syncretize the archaeological practice with the national identity working at different indigenous levels. The colonial framework is the biggest hindrance in promoting such an identity of pan-Indianness percolating down to all other indigenous levels.

We are still over-dependent on the textual evidences and somehow neglect the important archaeological findings for matters of vested interests. To further elaborate; let us look at the history-geography relationship in ancient India. If we look at it closely, the much talked about 'movement' seems to be contiguous from the neighbouring areas rather than movement from Europe to India. Thus, distinction between political boundaries and frontiers must be understood. Frontiers could have been crossed remaining in the subcontinent. It's only with the crossing of the political boundaries that the notion of 'foreign' comes to mind. The seals of Indus Valley Civilization (IVC), contrary to circular and cylindrical seals of Mesopotamia, were oblong or square signets. The objects depicted in the IVC are, thus, unique both in subject and in treatment though one cannot negate the evidences of contact between the two concurrent civilizations. This uniqueness provides a sense of identity different from the others. The uniqueness represents the linkages which spread across the whole subcontinent, i.e. the linkages of material culture across regions. Thus, there was no isolated zone and the regions interacted among themselves without the idea of any core or periphery.

The society was also multi-layered rather than being a socially hierarchical society. Craft, trade and agriculture and the communities involved interacted with each other promoting their own sense of identity and producing an intertwined identity at some level which was also very much indigenous and local. The Harappan pot as funerary objects, arranged around the head, suggests a belief in life after death which provides a local identity to the region based on their beliefs. The representation of all these nuances at the National Museum proves its worth in promoting the identity of being Indian in character and treatment. In fact, the mere existence of all these varieties renders the museum and its archaeological practice a national character.

Conclusion

Thus, by and large, we can trace and relate the identity through archaeology and its practicality in museums. However, museums in India need to go beyond the cultural aspect of the community. They need to look more into the socio-economic relationships between various communities of different regions. A multilineal perspective of the ancient Indian past should be developed to understand the history of the subcontinent in its own terms and framework.

Archaeology has been instrumental in defining history and museums have preserved the history for the ages to come. To have a more fruitful future, based on history, identities must be the cornerstone of studying the practices of humans across ages. Rethinking a sense of identity must be followed by ridiculing the colonial mindset of looking at things and perspectives as matters of subjective interests. Archaeology and museums must be intertwined to come up with such a broad framework of promoting

Indian identity at all possible levels.

The museums stand for the holistic presentation of various tribal and folk populations in the systematic way of socio-cultural, economic and technological aspects. At the same time, through its activities, museums must play a vital role in presenting the equality and dignity of all cultures in parallel developmental approach for preserving their cultural identity. This can be done only if the presentation is unbiased and not prejudiced towards any colonial or other motives. There is an urgent need for museums and community groups to come together to promote and preserve the unembodied cultural heritage. It is better to keep one's identity alive rather than adopting that of others.

References

Barker, Alex W. (2010). Exhibiting Archaeology: Archaeology and Museums. Annual Review of Anthropology, 39, 293-308.

Chakrabarti, Dilip K. (1982). The Development of Archaeology in the Indian Subcontinent. World Archaeology, 13 (3).

Singh, Kavita (2002). The Museum is National. India International Centre Quarterly, 29 (3 & 4).

Markham, S.F. and H. Hargreaves (1936). The Museums of India. London: The Museum Association.

Thakurta, Tapati Guha (1997). Sites of Art History: Canons and Expositions. Journal of Arts and Ideas, Special Issue.

Singh, Upinder (2004). The Discovery of Ancient India: Early Archaeologists and the Beginning of Archaeology. New Delhi: Permanent Black.

Pradhan, V. Ashok (2013). Indian Museums in Community Identity and Development: A Critical Study. International journal of Science Engineering and advance Technology, p. 25.

Accessed online at www.ijseat.com/index.php/ijseat/article/download/4/4.

Endnotes

1. Alex W. Barker (2010. Exhibiting Archaeology: Archaeology and Museums", Annual Review of Anthropology. 39, 293-308, p. 295.

2. Upinder Singh (2004). The Discovery of Ancient India: Early Archaeologists and the Beginning of Archaeology. New Delhi: Permanent Black, p. xv.

3. Ibid, p. 200.

4. Ibid, p. 205

5. Ibid, p. 291.

6. Ibid, p. 238.

7. V. Ashok Pradhan (2013). Indian Museums in Community Identity and Development: A Critical Study. International journal of Science Engineering and advance Technology, p. 25. Accessed online at www.ijseat.com/index.php/ijseat/article/download/4/4.

8. Ibid.

9. Kavita Singh (2002). The Museum is National. India International Centre Quarterly, 29 (3 & 4), pp. 176-196.

10. S.F. Markham and H. Hargreaves (1936). The Museums of India. London: The Museum Association, p. 99.

11. Tapati Guha-Thakurta (1997). Sites of Art History: Canons and Expositions. Journal of Arts and Ideas, Special Issue.

12. Dilip K. Chakrabarti (1982). The Development of Archaeology in the Indian Subcontinent. World Archaeology, 13 (3), pp. 326-344.

13. Ibid, p. 336.

CHAPTER - THIRTEEN

Journey towards Modern India: Indira Priyadarshini Gandhi the Creator of Modern India

Ashu J

"A nation's strength ultimately consists in what it can do on its own, and not in what it can borrow from others."

~ Indira Gandhi

Indian history was radically transformed with the emergency of the British East India Company. Even after the independence it was very challenging for the Indians to choose their leader who had the potential to transform India into a better place for living and livelihood and it was thus at that time during 1966 when India find it's so called the first women and third Prime Minister – Indira Gandhi. Indira was the daughter of the first Prime Minister Pandit Jawaharlal Nehru. Priyadarshini name was given to her in an interview by Rabindranath Tagore and thus she came to be popularly known as Indira Priyadarshini Gandhi. She was very dynamic, determined and the only female Prime Minister of India with inbuilt courage to put forth India into self-sufficient, self-reliance, peaceful as well as to make nation free from poverty. Before holding the office she was elected as Congress President in 1959 and this was her stepping stone which eventually landed herself as the Prime Minister of India. She served as Prime Minister from 1966 – 1977 and then again from 1980 until her assassination in 1984.

She was known for her political mercilessness and unprecedented centralisation of power, thus making it difficult to describe her contribution towards the formation of modern India. Although talking precisely about her contribution to the Indian nation which will not rest in few lines. She was successful in making India what we see today. She went to war with Pakistan in support of the independence movement and war of independence in East Pakistan, today popularly known as Bangladesh. Not only war against independence, she also made instrument in getting the Communist led Kerala State Government dismissed in 1959. Both the incidents indicate courageous acts during her tenure. She made a limit less change including making of her own faction within congress party and managed to retain most of the congress MP's on her side. One of the biggest achievement of Indira Gandhi was after been elected in 1971 to her decisive victory in the Indo-Pakistan War of 1971, that led to the formation of independent Bangladesh. She was hailed as *"Goddess Durga"* by opposition leader Atal Bihari Vajpayee.

She was well known for her foreign, domestic and economic policies. Precisely looking into the foreign polices of Gandhi, it was not restrict within India and its neighbour it also included South Asia, Middle East, Asia Pacific as well as Africa. During 1971, Gandhi intervened in the Pakistan Civil War in support of East Pakistan. Gandhi was recognized as the contributor to the independence of Bangladesh by Prime Minister Sheikh Mujibur Rahman. It can be clearly evident from the fact that Gandhi enjoys the highest state award posthumously for her outstanding contribution to the country's independence by Government of Bangladesh. She also maintained a good relationship with Sri Lanka. One of the most important foreign policy of her is said to be Operation Meghdoot which resulted in the victory of India during Siachen conflict against Pakistan. Another example of her diplomatic view and efficiency can be seen in managing the tension between the India and Iran during Pakistan war.

Southeast Asia also witnesses a major development in the form of foreign policies adopted by Gandhi by forming Association of Southeast Asian Nations (ASEAN). Nevertheless Gandhi was habile in reshaping the image between Commonwealth of Nations and liberal views of British colonial policies in East Africa. After Gandhi became Prime Minister, diplomatic and economic relations with the states which supported Indian during the Sino-Indian war were expanded in a good manner. Indian origin settled in Africa was also benefited with the foreign policy of Gandhi when she declared them as "Ambassadors of India". Foreign and domestic policy successes in the 1970s enabled Gandhi to rebuild India's image in the eyes of the different nations.

Despite the foreign policies Gandhi also paved way to the different economic policies in order to boost the Indian economy. She adopted different kinds of both aggressive and non-aggressive measures in order to tackle the challenges faced by the Indian economy, thus S. K. Datta Ray describe her as "a master of rhetoric.....often posture than policy". Among them one of the most important and effective economic measure was "Garibi Hatao" which means Remove Poverty which eventually became an iconic motto of the Indian National Congress in the later years. Apart from that she wanted the upliftment of rural and urban poor, women, untouchables in India, due to which she also came to be popularly known Indira Amma or Mother Indira.

Despite adopting active foreign and domestic policies, she always inherited a weak and troubled economic measure. She always remained so vulnerably dependent on aids and painstakingly began in building up substantial foreign exchange reserves continuously. Even after been dependent on aids, she began a new course by launching the fourth year plan in 1969 where she targeted growth rate at 5.7% with the goal of stability and progressive achievement of self-reliance. Although she was not very much successful in delivering with what she had imagined for the Indian economy. And this ultimately resulted in the failure of her party. But this failure was not permanent and this can be felt in her desire by regaining the throne in 1980 by winning by-election from Chikamagalur constituency to the Lok Sabha right after the state of emergency in 1975-1977.

Gandhi was determined and a confident women and this was evident from her hope and passion even after losing drastically with her economic measures adopted to boost Indian economy. For insistence, she initiated policies that were adopted by her father, Jawaharlal Nehru to deal with India's food problems. Apart from this with the failures in both fourth and fifth year plan, she came up with new and effective sixth year plan where she was able to make successful entry in putting India into a economically stable and reliable to a greater extend. Other important achievement includes the formation of the nationalized banking system which in paper she titled as "stray thoughts on bank nationalisation". In 1969, Gandhi moved to nationalise 14 major commercial banks. After the nationalization of banks, the branches of the public sector banks in India rose approximately by 800 percent in deposits and advance took a huge jump by 11,000 percent thus, resulting in rise of bank branches from about 8,200 to 62,000 approx. The really success was when Jayaprakash Narayan, who became famous for leading the opposition to Gandhi in 1970, was solid in praising her for nationalization of banks. Furthered with the success of nationalization process she precedes with the same strategy of nationalising the coal, steel, refining, cotton textiles and insurance industries.

Another painstaking move taken by Gandhi was to protect employment and also to protect the interest of the organised labourers. She believed in unity and the spirit of nationalism and for the same she managed the separation of the Hindi speaking southern half of Punjab which became a separate state, Haryana. Apart from that she usually made brilliant decision in the form of declaring Chandigarh as a Union Territory which is to be shared as a capital by both Punjab and Haryana in order to eliminate any threat. We can say that nationalism was in her blood and it was true when in 1972, Gandhi granted statehood to Meghalaya, Manipur and Tripura, while the North-East Frontiers Agency was declared a Union Territory and renamed as Arunachal Pradesh. The transition to the statehood for these territories was successfully overseen by her administration. This was followed by further annexation of Sikkim in 1975.

Indira Gandhi was not just merely a Prime Minister; she also took active part in social reforms as well. One such reform was towards the equality under the Gandhi's administration. Gandhi was the only one who questioned the continued existence of a privy purse for Indian monarchs. Gandhi claimed that only "clear vision iron will and the strictest discipline" can remove poverty. Gandhi was even praised in her decision in 1967 when Gandhi made a constitutional amendment that guaranteed the de facto use of both Hindi and English as official language of India, when the problem arises in making decision regarding the national language of India. Gandhi thus put herself forward as a leader with a pan-Indian vision. Gandhi wanted to change the overall look of India thus; she carried out the vision of her father cum former Premier of India Jawaharlal Nehru. Gandhi nurtured the vision of Nehru on establishing stable and secure interest from those of the nuclear superpower in order to make India among one of the member into the nuclear power holding nations. This program was matured in 1974, when Dr. Raja Ramanna delineated Gandhi that India had the ability to test its very first nuclear weapon. In 1974, India was able to conduct a successful underground nuclear test at Indian Army Pokhran Test Range near desert village of Pokhran in Rajasthan, which was unofficially coded with name "Smiling Buddha". Although this test created tensions for India, when the Prime Minister of Pakistan, Zulfikar Ali Bhutto replied to the successful test as "Indian hegemony" to intimidate Pakistan and adding further that "hum ghaas kha lay gay magar nuclear power ban k rhe gay (we would eat grass but would surely achieve nuclear power). But Indira Gandhi was tactically able to manage such tensions brought by the neighbouring nation/s.

To conclude it can be said that Indira Priyadarshini Gandhi was not only successful in her political and social career but also was successful in delivering a self-sufficient, self-reliant and stable India. We can say that Gandhi's achievements were once the backbone to the Indian nation and even it is felt that we are still continuing with some of her amendments even today. Not only her political, economic, social, domestic and foreign policies were badass, she also was one of the most popular faces between the poor, women and untouchable people. For instance, when Gandhi was arrested in response to the state of emergency, Indira Gandhi's supporters hijacked an Indian Airlines jet and demanded for her immediate release. This incident not only indicates the zeal of the thousands of people who supported her but also shows the image and respect for the Gandhi in each and every corner of the nation. Even after facing such crucial, challenging and worse situations within her tenure, she was utmost vigilant and unflinching. She remained role model to the women not only during that time but also she is still seen as one of the role model by women even today.

India lost such a brilliant and energetic leader Indira Gandhi on 31st October 1984, when she was shot to death by her two bodyguards', Satwant Singh and Beant Singh with their service weapons. Mercilessly, Beant Singh shot her three times using his side-arm while Satwant singh fired 30 rounds. Kehar Singh was later arrested for conspiracy in the attack. Despite taking her into the hospital after the shot at 09:30 AM to All Indian Institute of Medical Science, she was declared death at 02:20 PM after conducting several operations. Doctors reported there were 31 bullets were fires out of which 23 had passed through her body while 7 were trapped inside her. Gandhi's assassination was a shock for the people and it will always remain as a black mark in history. Thousands of thousands gathered to funeral ceremony and a live funeral telecast was made both domestically and internationally as a tribute to such a wonderful leader that put forth India into the global status. Gandhi was cremated on 3rd November near Raj Ghat and is today known as Shakti Sthala. Last but not the least Indira Gandhi was really a "Shakti" (meaning power) for the nation.

References

Katherine Frank (2010). Indira: the life of Indira Nehru Gandhi. UK: HarperCollins.

Meena Agrawal (2005). Indira Gandhi. New Delhi: Diamond Pocket Books.

Pranay Gupte (2012). Mother India: A Political Biography of Indira Gandhi. New Delhi: Penguin Books.

Pupul Jayakar (1997). Indira Gandhi: A Biography. New Delhi: Penguin Books.

Yogendra Kumar Malik (1988). India: The Years of Indira Gandhi. Netherlands: Brill Publishers.

Contributors

Ms. Apeksha Gandotra is an M.Phil. History student at University of Delhi. She's a Researcher who works in the field related to the development of research in Arts and Humanities. Her main research focus is on writing history with special reference to Mirabai.

Mr. Ashu J is working as Research Assistant in Department of Political Science, Maharaja Agrasen College at the University of Delhi, New Delhi. He formerly worked as Junior Project Fellow at DEAA, NCERT, New Delhi and Research Assistant at Cluster Innovation Centre, University of Delhi, New Delhi. He is an Editorial Reviewer of Research Journal of Humanities and Social Sciences, A & V Publication, Raipur. He served as an Intern at National Museum, New Delhi and Rajya Sabha Television (RSTV). He did his Masters in History with specialization in Ancient Indian History from Hans Raj College, University of Delhi. After his post-graduation he did Reprography Course from National Archives of India, New Delhi; Art Appreciation from National Museum Institute, New Delhi and Antiquity Trafficking and Art Crime from University of Glasgow, United Kingdom. He his published book is *"Lineage of Aśoka: Brāhmi, Dhamma and Edicts"*. His other published articles include: *Comparing Rāmāyaṇa of Valmiki and Kampan Ahalya's Episode*, New Delhi, 2016; *Understanding Delhi during 1803 - 1860*, Raipur, 2017 and *Reflection of Aśoka - His Idea of Dhamma in Pillar Edict Seven*, Raipur, 2018.

Mr. Bitumani Tahbildar has completed his B.E. degree from Annamalai University and MBA from Guwahati University. Being a pure science student, his appetency toward the better understanding and knowledge of ancient past, culture and civilization, he is currently pursuing his Master of Arts degree in History from K.K. Handique State University. He developed his research interests on studying popular religions and art depiction through religion.

Ms. Kanika Gupta is currently pursuing her PhD on the topic '*Yakṣī Cult in Early Mauryan to Kuṣāṇa Sculpture*' at School of Arts and Aesthetics, Jawaharlal Nehru University, Delhi. She completed her post-graduation in Art History and Aesthetics from Faculty of Fine Arts, Maharaja Sayajirao University of Baroda, Gujarat in 2012. Since then she has worked on several art and research projects like 'accessioning and documentation of Ananda Coomaraswamy and Kapila Vatsyayan personal collections for the Archives of Indira Gandhi National Centre for the Arts, Delhi' and content writing for thirty-five modules on 'History of Indian Sculpture' for e-pathshala, Online Post Graduate Diploma Course, Ministry of Human Resource Department (MHRD), Government of India, among others.

Mr. Prabira Sethy teaches Political Science in Department of Political Science, Maharaja Agrasen College at University of Delhi. He has experience of more than 10 years of teaching and still continues to nurture the young generation. However, he has been involved in several book making process by contributing his valuable chapter for the following books: *Women and Rural Development*, *Academic and Activist Perspectives on Biodiversity and Climate Change*, Vol. I and *India in Global Affairs: Changing Dynamics and Emerging Role*. His published articles includes: *Tribal Displacement and Resettlement: Effective Safeguards*, New Delhi, 2008; *Strengthening Molestation Law for Women's Safety in India*, New Delhi, 2008; *Sex Education: The Sooner The Better*,

New Delhi, 2008; *Reforming Judiciary: The Issue of Selection and Removal of Judges in India*, New Delhi, 2009; *A Road to Electoral Reform: A Study of the Impact of 'None-of-the-Above' (NOTA) Votes in Delhi Legislative Assembly Elections -2015*, Mumbai, 2014; *Salient Features of the British General Elections -2015*, Maharashtra, 2016 and *India's Candidature for Permanent Membership of the United Nations Security Council: A Long Road Ahead*, New Delhi, 2017

Dr. Rajeev Kumar is Research Associate at Maharaja Agrasen College, University of Delhi. He is also currently teaching at the Non-Collegiate Women's Education Board, University of Delhi as Assistant Professor. Prior to this, he was teaching at Satyawati College, University of Delhi. He also worked as Research Assistant at the Centre for Land Warfare Studies (CLAWS), New Delhi in the year 2016. He holds a Ph.D. Degree from the School of International Studies, Jawaharlal Nehru University (JNU), New Delhi. He has co-edited a book titled India-Nepal: Seven Decades of Trust and Partnership. He has also contributed several research papers and articles in academic journals and magazines. His research interests include history of South Asia, with particular reference to India-Nepal relations.

Ms. Srotoswini Borah is an alumnus of University of Delhi and has completed her Masters of Arts in History with specialization in Ancient Indian History. She's an independent Researcher who works in the field related to the development of research in Arts and Humanities. Her published articles includes: *Jaina Religion and Their Heritage in Bihar*, Raipur, 2017 and *'Nagas': The Religious Pantheon of Ancient India*, Raipur, 2018.

Mr. TCA Achintya is presently an M.Phil scholar in the Department of History at the University of Delhi, focusing on the 19th century, in particular on the impact of British Political and Constitutional History, Parliamentary Politics and Global Events on Legislations governing India. He is a student of Modern History at the Department of History, University of Delhi. His broader interests include exploring Early Colonial Indian History, though he has also done some work on Ancient Indian Epic Literature and on Education Policy in India. His other research interests includes Global History, Political History, Constitutional and Legislative Histories, Modern Indian History.

Ms. Vandana Rana is a Lecturer at Lingaya's Lalita Devi Institute of Management and Sciences. She did her Masters of Arts and Bachelors of Arts in History from University of Delhi. She also did her B.Ed from IP University. She did her short term program in records management from National Archives of India. It was during her degree program she developed her research interest in comparative analysis of written and oral history. She is keen to unlock the manifold aspects of history.

Index

A

Agañña Sutta vii, 29, 30, 33, 36, 55, 61, 64

Al-biruni 105

Alexander Cunningham 128

Ancient History vii, 1, 7, 13

Arthaśāstra 66, 72, 74

Aryasatyani 22

Ashtadhyayi 17

Asoka 26, 128

Assalayana Sutta 42

Association of Southeast Asian Nations 148

Astangika Marga 22

Atranjikhera 16

Avidhamma Pitaka 22

Ayas 16, 17

Ayovikara 17

B

Banaprastha 19

Boucher 79

Brahminical texts 17

Buddhism 2

Buddhist Samgha 26

C

Cakkavatti Sihanada Sutta 53

Chalcolithic period 14, 15

Cleitus 97

D

Dhamma 21, 26, 36, 37, 39, 50, 51, 52, 53, 54, 61, 62, 63, 153

Dīdārgañj Caurī viii, 3, 66, 68

Dīdārgañj yak☒ī 66, 67, 69

Dīgha Nikāya vii, 2, 3, 29, 30, 31, 33, 38, 44, 53, 55, 60

Dipavamsa 128

Dugdhadharini 79

E

East India Company 134

Eightfold Paths 22. *See also* Astangika Marga

F

Fa-Hien 129

French Revolution 5, 117

G

Gahapati 41, 51

Ga☒ikā 71, 76

Genghis Khan 92, 97, 98, 103

Gosala Mankhaliputta 20

Gupta Empire 93

H

Han Dynasty 93

Harappan civilization 15, 140, 142

Hastinapur 16

Hinayanists 25

Hiuen-Tsang 129

Hulegu Khan 100

I

Indira Priyadarshini Gandhi 6, 146, 151

Iron Age vii, 2, 14, 15, 16, 17, 18

K

Kāmasūtra 66

Kapilavatthuin 29

Karmafalas 19

Kharoshthi 128

Khwarazm Empire 94

Kshatriyas 19, 31, 38, 41, 43, 44, 47

Kulaputtas 23

L

La Marseillaise 113

Licchavis 62, 73

Lumbini 20

M

Macedonian Empire 97

Magadha 26

Mahasammata 39

Mahavamsa 128

Mahayana Buddhism 27

Mahayanists 25

Majjhima Nikāya 45, 56

Malwa region 17

Manusmriti 72

Markham-Hargreaves Report 138

Mathurā Parkham yak☒a 70

Medieval History 3

Megalithic culture 15

Modern History viii, 4, 111, 155

Moksha 2

Mongol 4

N

Nā⊠yaśāstra 66

Nikāyas 21, 30, 36, 37, 39, 43, 46, 47, 63

O

Operation Meghdoot 147

P

Palaeolithic 9, 10, 11, 13, 18

Pali Nikāyas 39

Parmenion 97

Pā⊠aliputra 66, 70, 71, 76

Picasso 79

Pleistocene Epoch 9

Priyadarshini 146

Proto historical period 12

Ptolemy 97

R

Rathalatthi Jataka 39

Roman Empire 93

S

Sannyasa 19

Sassanid dynasty 101

Śatapatha Brāhma⊠a 17

Siddhartha Gautama 20, 21, 29, 30

Sramanas movement 20

Subutai 97

Sudras 23

Sutta Nipata 17, 23

Sutta Pitaka 21, 30

T

Taittiriya Samhita 17

Tesakuna Jataka 32

Turkish Empire 14

U

Upper Gangetic valley 16

V

Vajji Janapada 73

Vessa 36, 38

W

Wheel of Law 29

Y

Yajurveda 17

www.ingramcontent.com/pod-product-compliance
Lightning Source LLC
Chambersburg PA
CBHW030656230426
43665CB00011B/1111